DATE DUE

MAR 13 2012	
ILL 10/12	
—	

HISTORY *of*

OLYMPIC GAMES

Ancient and Modern

by

HUGH HARLAN

ILLUSTRATED

Together With Official Olympic
and World Records and
Proposed Program of
Xth Olympiad

——

Published by
BUREAU OF ATHLETIC RESEARCH
LOS ANGELES
U. S. A.

First Printing, May, 1931, 10,000 copies
Second Printing (Revised and Enlarged), April, 1932,
50,000 copies

HISTORY OF OLYMPIC GAMES, ANCIENT AND MODERN

PRINTED BY ART JONES PRINTING CO.
LOS ANGELES, CALIFORNIA

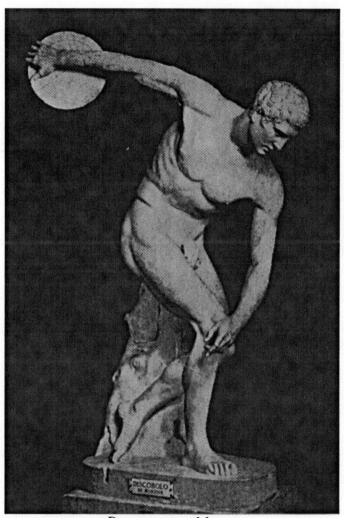

DISCOBOLUS OF MYRON

This copy of the famous discus thrower is in the Vatican at Rome. It idealizes the perfection of all-round physical development characteristic of Grecian athletes of the Golden Age of Olympia.

TABLE OF CONTENTS

ILLUSTRATIONS

PREFACE

Psychologists have long held it axiomatic that the play life of a race reveals, to a greater degree than any other activity, its inherent mental and physical characteristics.

In no other activity does *homo sapiens* display as high a grade of sportsmanship, fair play and co-operation in relation to his fellows as he does in his games.

If it is true that the spirit of play is indicative of a high order of intelligence and that it liberates the soul of man then it is time that serious effort should be made to interpret the relationship between man and his play life.

That field of study lies beyond the scope of the present volume n fact but not in theory.

Very properly any consideration of the subject must be based upon the Grecian ideal of sports as exemplified in the ancient Olympic Games. The remarkable vitality of this ideal as expressed in the purest form of sportsmanship of the participants as well as the art and literature of the Golden Age of Greece is without parallel in recorded history.

In outlining briefly the history of the ancient and modern Olympic games this volume is offered with the hope that it will serve the reader as a primer which will stimulate him to a further study of the subject. The bibliography at the end of this book will furnish those interested with a list of books that will carry them into new and fascinating fields of research.

With grateful appreciation the author acknowledges the assistance of Prof. J. Tarbotton Armstrong, Mr. Dean Cromwell and Mr. George T. Davis in preparing this volume.

H. H.

The truth is that we are far more likely to underrate the originality of the Greeks than to exaggerate it, and we do not always remember the very short time they took to lay down the lines scientific inquiry has followed ever since.—JOHN BURNET.

———

To get rid of one's ignorance, to see things as they are, and by seeing them as they are to see them in their beauty, is the simple and attractive ideal which Hellenism holds out.—MATTHEW ARNOLD.

CHAPTER I

ANCIENT GREECE

History is the story of the way in which man has learned and is still learning, how to live: of how through long centuries he has sought to satisfy the practical needs of his body, the questioning of his mind, and the searching of his spirit.

Dorothy Mills.

IN GREECE, the ancient and honored cradle of tolerant and civilized intellectualism, were born the Olympic Games. Their origin is buried in antiquity but their idealism is as pertinently desirable now as the day they sprang into existence. They were predicated on the theory that the body of man is of equal importance with his intellect and that only by their mutual discipline and co-ordination is he glorified.

Tradition has it that the games were inaugurated as a religious festival in honor of the Grecian god, Zeus. But their significance and influence can not be measured by the narrow yardstick of religious ceremony. The Greeks were too broadminded and cosmopolitan to restrain their activities, mental and physical, with the deadening dogma of cant.

Because modern civilization is based largely upon ancient Grecian civilization our attention is directed almost entirely to the men who were the founders of intellectualism. In our glorification of Homer, Pericles, Aristophanes, Socrates, Xenophon, Plato, Aristotle, Demosthenes, Praxiteles, Euclid, Pindar, Anaxagoras, Pausanias, and many other Grecian Greats we have overlooked the conditions which made it possible for such men to perform their wonders.

It cannot be gainsaid that the Olympic games were one of the chief factors that contributed to the greatness of ancient Greece. The strong influence they exerted over Hellas (the name by which the Greeks called their own country) cannot be overestimated and will be dwelt on as we progress further into this history.

To obtain an intelligent grasp of the idea back of the Olympic games, for what they stood and how they flavored Grecian life and conduct, it is necessary that we digress for the moment and make a brief survey of ancient Greece.

In the cloudy dawn of traditional history, 1500—1200 B.C., the Greeks, a savage and nomadic Nordic people, surged southwards from the interior of Europe into the Balkan peninsula. They had fair skin, blond hair and were long of limb and extremely strong and agile.

So far as we have been able to trace them they originated in Central Europe, which was also the breeding place of other Caucasian races. Philologists (language scholars) find that the root stocks of Grecian words are similar to those of English, German, French, Spanish, Italian, Russian and Persian, hence they assume these races were at one time intermingled. As a group these races are known variously as the Caucasian, Nordic or Aryan peoples.

The Greeks evidently came into the Balkan peninsula in three successive invasions for we find three dominant varia- tions of speech, namely, the Ionic, Æolic and the Doric.

Here these barbarians found a highly developed civiliza- tion, headed by the city of Cnossos on the island of Crete. This civilization they conquered and later assimilated as the basis of the Grecian civilization with which we are acquainted.

They mixed with the conquered Mediterranean peoples to such an extent that it is doubtful if the Ionic and Æolic tribes in the course of time did not lose their original racial characteristics to a certain degree.

This cannot be surmised concerning the Doric tribes, however, for they penetrated into the Peloponnesus to emerge into recorded history as the Spartans, a division that seemed best fitted to uphold the traditions of the race.

The Doric invasion was the third and last of the succes- sive waves of barbarians into the Balkan peninsula. This tribe was not only the most powerful but also, after centuries of strife, proved itself the most virile of the Grecian peoples.

After these various migrations and settlements we find the Greeks, having absorbed and perfected the art of writing, emerging into the dawn of history about 700—600 B.C.

Ethnologists (students of the human race) tell us that the physical properties or topography of the land in which any race dwells exert a strong influence upon the development of that national group. Consult now the map of ancient Greece on page 12, as salient facts are pointed out to you.

You will observe that Greece, not a large country, may be divided roughly into three sections; the northern, chiefly mountainous; the central, also mountainous but with many hill-locked valleys; and the southern division, a peninsula, known as the Peloponnesus, which is likewise mountainous with numerous isolated valleys. In size Greece is but a trifle larger than the state of Maryland.

You will also note that due to its narrowness and extremely irregular coast line all sections are comparatively close to the sea. Of the total area of Greece almost one-third is rocky and mountainous, hence unfit for cultivation. The valleys are, of course, cultivated but the soil is not particularly fertile.

The chief agricultural products of the ancient Greeks were wheat, barley, olives and grapes. The olive tree was considered sacred. Its fruit and oil were everyday necessities. Grapes were chiefly made into wine, yet the Greeks were a temperate race.

The Grecian summers were tempered by cool Mediterranean winds so it was seldom extremely hot. The winters were not severe and there were but few violent storms.

Taking into consideration all these conditions we can readily perceive their influence upon the Greeks. The mountainous districts developed a hardy, independent spirit. In the dwellers of the valleys, being almost entirely shut off from the inhabitants of nearby valleys, was also fostered

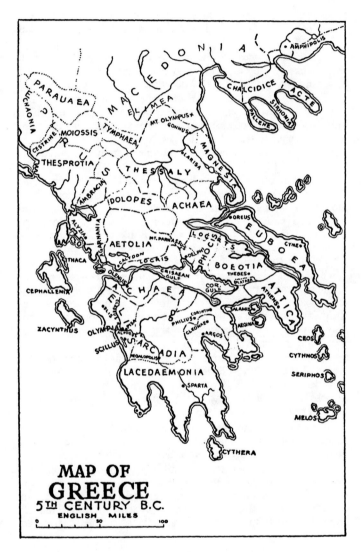

MAP OF
GREECE
5TH CENTURY B.C.
ENGLISH MILES
0   50   100

independence. Then proximity to the sea made the entire race "sea-conscious," and sea-rovers are ever freedom-lovers.

Add to all these facts the meager productiveness of the soil and we begin to get an insight into the Grecian characteristics of frugality and moderation. Lastly we consider the mild climate which made it necessary for the Greeks to devote but a small portion of their time for the purpose of securing storm-proof shelter and clothing and we must realize that these conditions permittted and were conducive to clear thinking.

These are some of the physical reasons why the Greeks were the first and therefore possibly the greatest free thinkers. When we contemplate the appalling ignorance prevalent in the world today, we can but marvel at the intense curiosity of the ancient Greeks in questioning all things, and but admire the clearness of mind and courage of intellect they displayed in their passionate search for truth.

Hence is was as staunch exponents of freedom of physical and mental activities, as clear-thinking searchers after truth, as lovers of beauty in nature and as disciples of self-control the ancient Greeks laid the foundation of much that we hold priceless in our modern civilization.

Obviously it would be outside the bounds of truth to say the physical properties of Greece, such as the topography, the climate and relative fertility of the soil, were alone responsible for the greatness that was Grecian. These conditions were the favorable environment which fostered the growth of Hellas. The Greeks must have had, and did have, as has already been pointed out, a strong hereditary influence derived from a clean-limbed, open-minded, rugged and vigorous ancestry.

We know this to be true, for while the Greeks were growing in knowledge and ability other races which had been cradled upon the shores of the Mediterranean Sea and who lived contemporaneously with and in practically the same environment as the Greeks, did little or nothing of lasting benefit for on-coming generations.

Here we have a country made up of numerous small and independent cities and states, many of which were shut off from their neighbors by natural barriers. These cities and states were extremely jealous of their rights and freedom and naturally such a condition could lead to nothing except misunderstandings.

Misunderstandings lead to hatred and thus were engendered wars. So we find the ancient Greeks almost constantly engaged in war and rumors of war. It was state against state, city against city, coalition against alliance, an eternal warfare for supremacy.

The Greeks maintained no standing armies and they had no military class, hence it was necessary that every Greek citizen between the ages of eighteen and sixty be prepared to engage in combat without a moment's notice. That meant he must ever be in excellent physical condition. It now becomes somewhat obvious as to why the Greeks took to systematic physical training and why athletic festivals flourished in every city and state.

Paradoxically enough we find that while the Greeks apparently engaged in athletic contests as a means of keeping physically fit for instant participation in warfare, they actually were not so concerned with the prowess of athletes as they were with the spirit of fair play engendered in contests and the skill and finessé displayed by the contestants.

With the foregoing conditions in mind as a background or "scenery" for our review we can now place the Olympic games in the center of our mental "stage" for intelligent investigation with everything in proper perspective.

CHAPTER II

ORIGIN OF OLYMPIC GAMES

It is not the least of the many debts which
we owe Heracles that by instituting the Olympic
games he restored peace and good will to a land
torn asunder by war and faction and wasted by
pestilence.—Lysias, *Panegyric.*

THE ANSWER TO the question, "Who originated the Olympic
games?" is simply this, "No one."

What we mean is that their origin cannot be credited to
any one individual, nor for that matter, to any small group
of individuals.

The Olympic games were an outgrowth of minor athletic
festivals held in various localities of ancient Greece. These
athletic festivals were in turn the outgrowth of many natural
conditions, including the heredity, environment, religion and
athletic spirit of the Grecian tribes, plus the fact, as we have
already read, that they had to be ever prepared for instant
participation in warfare.

The Greeks themselves did not know who started the
Olympic games. And to cover up their ignorance they said
their gods originated them.

The Greek traditional stories of the beginning of the
Olympic games are various. One account says the first contest to be staged on the Olympian plains was when Zeus
wrestled Cronus for control of the world. Still another relates that Apollo there engaged in a boxing contest with
Ares. A third credits their origin to the Idæan Heracles who
was said to have instituted them as a means of bringing together in a common cause the warring Grecian tribes, this
latter theory was held by Lysias and Pausanias.

Pindar, however, in a theory more in accord with logic, ascribes their origin to funeral games in honor of Pelops, a tribal chieftain. His story runs to the effect that Œnomaus, father of Hippodameia, was once the ruler of Olympia. Thither came Pelops as a suitor for the hand of this beautiful maiden. But Œnomaus had a quaint practice of challenging all his daughter's suitors to a chariot-race and killing those whom he defeated. Thirteen suitors had preceded Pelops and had met death in their search for love. Pelops, through a neat bit of knavery, secured the assistance of Myrtilus, charioteer of Œnomaus, who disabled his master's chariot to such a degree that Pelops won the race, killed the father, married the girl and annexed the kingdom. Pelops then erected monuments in the Altis to his accomplishments, and after his death his tomb was placed there.

Pindar goes on to say that Heracles, the son of Zeus, having returned from his victory over Augeas, instituted the Olympic games as a funeral celebration before the tomb of Pelops in the Altis. "He (Heracles) measured a sacred grove for the Father," says Pindar[1], "and having fenced round the Altis marked the bounds thereof. There he set apart the choicest of the spoil for an offering from the war and sacrificed and ordained the fifth year feast." Then he names the winners of the foot-race, wrestling and boxing matches, and the chariot-races. There seems to be some evidence to substantiate his narrative as excavators found votive offerings of horses and chariot models under the foundations of the Heræum which Dr. Doerpfeld ascribes to the tenth or eleventh centuries B.C.

We first see Olympia, then, as the scene of funeral games which were held before the tomb of Pelops. The ancient tribes gathered there at stated intervals to worship their hero in a festival and to consult their oracle in the rustling of leaves. These tribes were roughly known as the Pisatæ, chiefly because of the nearness of Pisa, their home city, to Olympia.

---

[1] Pindar, *Olympian*, xi.64

But there was a constant struggle for supremacy among these tribes. Newcomers were pushing into the Peloponnesus to conquer or be conquered. The story of their heroic struggles are dramatically narrated in the *Odyssey*. The powerful Dorians seem to have been the last to invade the Peloponnesus, and after many years of bitter struggling they assumed complete control.

During these years of warfare the prehistoric Olympic games languished and all but died out despite the attempts of the Pisatans to maintain them under their control. The rekindling of the athletic spirit of Olympia was said to be due largely to the advice of the Delphic oracle who advised their re-establishment as a means of bringing peace and understanding to the warring tribes.

While the Greeks were split up into independent and jealous cities and states they had many things in common which made for national unity.

They called themselves by a common name, Hellenes, spoke a common language and had the same gods. Their native land was known as Hellas. It was not until after the Roman conquest that they were called Greeks. The Olympic games also exerted a strong influence in promoting national unity. But throughout their early history the Grecian tribes were torn between an intense spirit of individualism and Panhellenic idealism, a condition reflected in the rise and fall of the pre-historic Olympic games.

Lycurgus of Sparta, Iphitus, king of Elis, and Cleosthenes, king of Pisa, were said to have been instrumental in reviving the games. The laws of the athletic festival were inscribed on a discus together with the names of the first two mentioned rulers. This discus was kept in the temple of Hera where it was seen by Pausanias[1]. In fact the names of Lycurgus and Iphitus were still discernible when Aristotle visited the games. The veracity of this story has not been established but at least the re-organization of the Olympic games by Iphitus and Cleosthenes (it is doubtful if Lycurgus

---

[1] Pausanias, v 20,1

figured in the re-organization) marks the emergence of the athletic festival into recorded history, 776 B.C.

Cities and states all over Greece held athletic contests. Because of convenient locations and traditions a few of these games grew into more prominence than others. Chief among these were the Pythian games held at Delphi, located at the base of Mt. Parnassus, about eighty miles northwest of Athens, which were dedicated to Apollo in memory of his killing of the Python; the Isthmian games held at Corinth, located about fifty miles west of Athens on the narrow neck of the Peloponnesus, in honor of Poseidon, god of the sea; and the Nemean games held in a cypress grove before the temple of the Nemean Zeus at a location half way between Philius and Cleonæ, about seventy-five miles west of Athens, to commemorate the slaying of the Nemean lion by Heracles.

While these festivals embraced a number of athletic contests they ran more to competitions in art, literature and music, and were of a decidedly more religious character than the Olympic games.

At first blush it may seem strange that Olympia ranked first in popularity as a Panhellenic festival over its rivals. Delphi, Corinth and Nemea were all closer to Athens, the population center of Greece, than Olympia.

Yet the very remoteness of Olympia put it in a class by itself. It caught the popular fancy because it best interpreted the life, ideals and activities of Panhellenic Greece.

The beginning of the ascendency of the Olympic games over other national festivals was first given official recognition during the reign of Solon, the law-giver, over Athens when he decreed that an Athenian victor in the Isthmian games was to be rewarded with a hundred drachmas while an Olympic winner was to receive five hundred.

The Olympic games were held once every four years and so important became the quadrennial athletic festivals that the Greeks reckoned time with them, calling the four year period elapsing between each meeting an Olympiad. The first recorded festival was held in 776 B.C., and they continued until 392 A.D., a span of 1168 years, ranking them as one of the longest lived of man-made institutions.

Major and minor athletic festivals seem to have been held in rotation. Quite often both athletes and spectators travelled from one to the other.

This succession of festivals may be likened to county and state fairs held in the United States. These are usually scheduled so that various concessions may play at them successively.

But here the comparison ends.

The competition at the Grecian festivals was amateur in character and the visitors not only came to view the games but also to listen to noted musicians, classic poets and philosophers.

In America, however, the automobile and horse racing is wholly professional and it would be difficult to imagine the average fair crowd listening to the teachings of sound philosophers, even if we were blessed with any.

Rather the American peasants throng into mechanical rides which are accompanied by the most barbaric music and patronize street fakers and shows of the most crude and vulgar types.

Olympia, the scene of the ancient Olympic games, is located in Elis on the western side of the Peloponnesus, approximately one hundred and twenty-five miles west of Athens and ten miles east of the Ionian Sea.

Ancient Olympia was a veritable garden of the gods. The tree-dotted plain was formed by the confluence of the Alpheus river (now known as the Ruphia) and the Cladeus river. The floor of the valley, wide and fertile, was practically level and surrounding it on three sides were tree-clad hills whose gently sloping inclines made it into a natural amphitheatre. During the period of the Olympic games the Alpheus was navigable past Olympia.

To the north of the plain of Olympia was a pine-covered conical hill, approximately four hundred feet high, which was known to the ancient Greeks as the Cronian hill. It was sacred to Cronus. At its base was a grove of wild olive trees, the sacred grove which gave the Altis its name.

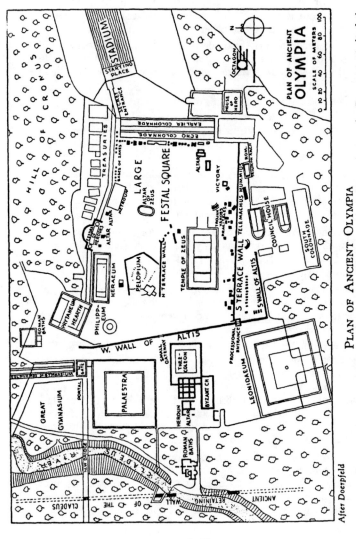

After Doerpfeld

PLAN OF ANCIENT OLYMPIA

This restored plan of Olympia is based upon its supposed condition during the Roman period of the second century A.D. The hippodrome was south of the Stadium, approximately where the octagon and direction arrow appear at the lower right-hand corner of the drawing. The restoration is a result of excavations conducted by the German government in the late seventies of the nineteenth century.

Apollo is reported to have said when he first saw beautiful Olympia, "Here I will make me a fair temple to be an oracle for men."

The site of Olympia is bounded on the south by the Alpheus river, on the east by the race courses, on the north by the Cronian hill and on the west by the Cladius river.

The first building to be erected at Olympia was probably the temple of Hera. Built, it is estimated, about 1000 B.C., one of its wooden columns was in evidence up to the time of Pausanias.

Another temple contained Phidias' marvelous statue of Zeus. Of heroic proportions, it was sculptured of pure ivory and gold. The form and face were moulded into wondrous beauty. Men saw the glory of sunshine on its brow and the gladness of summer skies in its face.

The games were held during the second or third full moon following the summer solstice, which made them fall usually in August, although the peculiarities of the Grecian calendar placed them occasionally in September. Either the 14th or 15th, the date of the full moon, seems to have been the central day of the festival which, according to the best authorities, lasted five days. The Greek day began at sunset and all sacrifices and religious ceremonies were required to be made before twelve o'clock noon.

In speaking of the Grecian observance of the Olympic games as being religious in character the reader is cautioned to differentiate between the meaning of religion as the Greeks knew it and as it is now construed.

This may seem a bit perplexing at first and it might be well to delve into its meaning for a moment so as to eliminate the possibility of misunderstanding the Greek character and the Olympic ideal.

The ancient Greeks were not religious in the sense that the modern world construes the term "religious." It is true they had many gods to whom sacrifices were made and of whom advice was asked. But it was not a particularly serious business with them. One can almost imagine the Greeks thumbing their noses even as they consulted their gods and oracles.

Greek gods left their places of abode and were presumed to mingle freely with the people. The ancient Greeks were essentially a race of "doers." Action was the keynote of their lives, as well as of their gods. One could almost say that their gods were glorified athletes.

The Israelite idea of a god sitting upon a throne in judgment of the peoples of the earth apparently never entered the Greek consciousness. To the Greeks, their gods and goddesses were playmates and comrades, more or less obviously made up of the imagery of what the strongest, wisest and most beautiful men and women should resemble.

Greek thinkers early looked with skepticism upon Grecian gods. Xenophanes was probably the first to discover that gods were created by men in their own image rather than by the reverse process.

True it was that the bulk of the Greeks were unable to keep up with the advanced or critical thinking of their philosophers. The impulse of the ignorant is ever to destroy or suppress that which they cannot, or will not, understand. Hence, many Greeks were banished, including Aristotle and Anaxagoras, and Socrates was condemned to death for their honest seeking after truth.

But the seed of rational thinking sown by the Grecian intellectualists blossomed for many centuries until the Roman conquest supplanted the word "reason" with that of "faith."

Tracing this line of thought further may enable us to better understand the rationalistic attitude of the Greeks towards life. Their gods were idealized athletes who had their own sports and games. They were the national heroes. As the Greeks gradually brought their gods down from the skies and into their everyday life of sports, war and other activities, it is easy to realize how they grew to idealize the victors of the Olympic games and make of them national heroes, supplanting to some extent the worship of gods.

The transition brought rational thinking to the Greeks in that they were thus led to glorify the deeds of men and women and to seek to approach perfection in human form and wisdom here and now rather than at some distant time and place.

No foreigners (barbarians, the Greeks called them) could enter Olympia as contestants, no foreign king could offer sacrifices to its gods. Hence, Olympia was exclusively Pan-hellenic, a bond that held the scattered members of Hellas in sympathetic and understanding contact. Only Greeks of pure Hellenic blood could participate in the games. And they must be free of any infraction of the law and be not guilty of neglecting to pay any penalty incurred to Zeus.

But these were the only requirements. Distinctions of class, rank, position or wealth were unknown. Thus Olympia was a potent leveller of class-consciousness and an influence for democracy.

The Greeks of the Homeric period wore the loin cloth when participating in athletics. This practice persisted in the early Olympic games, in fact until the festival of 720 B.C.

Curiously enough the abandonment of the loin cloth by Grecian athletes is said to have been caused by an accident. Pausanias[1] records that Orsippus of Megara, in Olympiad 15, accidentally dropped his loin cloth in the stadion race. Un-impeded by this bit of clothing he won the race in impressive fashion. The quick-witted Greeks, noting the advantage of running naked, thereafter discarded the loin cloth. An epi-gram, said to have been written by Simonides and inscribed on the tomb of Orsippus, commemorates this event.

Each contestant was required to train for ten months prior to the games. The last month of this training period must be spent at Elis under the guidance of the judges, known as the Hellanodicæ, who also had undergone a ten months' training period for their work.

The last month of training was severe and exacting. The judges disqualified those who appeared to be unable to com-pete in a competent fashion. At the close of this intensive preparatory work all the athletes were called before the Hellanodicæ who admonished them, according to Philostratus[2] as follows:

"If you have exercised yourself in a manner worthy of the Olympic games, if you have been guilty of no slothful or

[1] Pausanias. i.44   [2] Philostratus, Vit. Apoll. Tyan. v.43

ignoble act, go on with a good courage. You who have not so practiced, go whither you will."

The athletes and the Hellanodicæ, their period of train-ing completed, left Elis for Olympia a few days before the first day of the festival. With them went their trainers, horses and chariots, in fact the whole male population of the city. Two days were spent by the picturesque procession in the journey to Olympia.

If there was any competition on the first day it was only that for heralds and trumpeters, an event that was added to the festival in 396 B.C. The contestants were drawn up be-fore the statue of Zeus. A boar was then sacrificed to the god and, with their hands on its steaming entrails, the athletes swore that they had trained faithfully for ten months and that they would be fair and honest with all fellow contest-ants and not employ any unfair advantage to win.

The Hellanodicæ themselves swore in the same manner that they would render fair and honest decisions and would accept no bribes. They also at this time declared the eligibility of boys and colts to perform as such.

Following this ceremony the names of those athletes who had qualified were broadcast by heralds and their names written upon a large white board.

Thus, the day preceding the actual start of the games was spent in getting settled, swearing in the athletes, consulting oracles, making sacrifices and performing the many prelimi-naries necessary for the great athletic festival.

CHAPTER III

ANCIENT OLYMPIC EVENTS

He that overcometh hath, because of the
games, a sweet tranquility throughout his life for
evermore.   —*Pindar.*

IT IS ASTONISHING how much of our so-called modern thought
and activities were fathered by the ancient Greeks. To them
we must attribute not only many of our sports but also the
very names by which we designate them.

From the Greek word *athlon,* meaning "prize," come the
English words meaning "athlete" and "athletics," or the one
who competes or strives for a prize or honor.

Greek athletes performed entirely naked. The Grecian
word for "unclad" is *gymnos,* from which the English words
"gymnast," "gymnastic" and "gymnasium" were derived.

The Grecian *stadion,* a measure of length equal to 600
Olympic feet, which was also the name of the Olympic short
footrace, gives us "stadium," or the place where all kinds of
athletic contests are held.

The quoit which the Greeks used in the Olympic games
was known as a *diskos,* hence, our present word "discus." In
short, Grecian words not only enrich our literature but also
add much to our sport nomenclature.

It now becomes a matter of interest to make a survey of
the athletic events, paraphernalia and stadia of the ancient
Olympic games so that we can trace their development in our
modern games.

The race-course of the pre-historic man required but a
flat plot of ground over which the contestants ran to the
finish marked by some natural object such as a tree or rock.
For a longer race the contestants ran to or around the tree

and back to the starting line. Such a primitive race course can be seen in use today by boys in the lower grades of school and by the yokels of the hinterlands.

The Grecian stadia evolved from this primitive race course into a rectangular field on which both the starting line and the finish were marked by stone slabs and pillars. For the convenience of the spectators these stadia were laid out on terrain surrounded by gently sloping hills. As the years rolled by the ancient stadia became more and more elaborate with stone seats for the spectators and many acces-sories such as gymnasia and baths. These Grecian stadia are in sharp contrast to the modern ones, theirs being laid out in the form of a rectangle or parallelogram while ours are in the shape of an oval.

The stadium at Olympia was the most simple and una-dorned of any in ancient Greece. Prior to 450 B.C. the races were held within the Altis in front of the treasury terrace. Upon the completion of the first eastern colonnade, however, a new race track was cut at the foot of the Cronian hill in the form of a parallelogram. The sloping hillside of Cronus afforded room for from 20,000 to 30,000 spectators, where they sat on the ground or roamed about at will. The only seats provided were for the officials, the Hellanodicæ, and the priestess of Demeter Chamyne, the only woman privi-leged to see the games.

In size the Olympic race track or stadium was approxi-mately thirty-two yards wide by two hundred and thirty yards long. The course was enclosed by a low stone sill. Approximately a yard inside this sill was an open stone gutter in which drinking water ran for the benefit of both contestants and spectators.

Stone sills marked the starting line for foot races (Fig. 1). Those at Olympia were approximately eighteen inches wide and were set at both ends of the stadium to mark both the start and finish of the race-course. Parallel grooves about seven inches apart were cut on the top of the sill. They were obviously used to mark the place for the runners' feet, who started from an upright position. The grooves appear too shallow to serve as an aid in getting a quicker start.

Square sockets divided the sills at intervals of four feet. They evidently were provided for posts to mark each contestant's place at the start and also to serve as a marker around which each runner must race in the diaulos, or race of two stadia.

The two sills lie 192.27 meters apart and as the stadion race was calculated by the Greeks as being 600 Grecian feet, we obtain .32045 meters as the length of the Grecian foot.

At Olympia the classification of contestants included only men and boys. The age limit for boys seems to have been from seventeen to twenty years.

FIG. 1

This drawing shows a portion of the stone starting sill used at Olympia. These sills were approximately 18 inches wide and divided at intervals of 4 feet with square sockets for posts. Two parallel grooves 7 inches apart, were cut on the surface of the sill to mark the position of the runners' feet. These grooves were too shallow to serve as a means of getting a quick start.

Before the era of recorded history the games at Olympia were probably of a very primitive type consisting of foot races, with and without shields, and possibly wrestling and boxing. The length of the foot races in ancient Greece varied according to the stadium in which they were held. At Olympia, as we have already learned, the course was 192.27 meters (a trifle over 210 yards) long. Once down this course was called the stadion or stade-race. The race of twice the length of the course was known as the diaulos. The long race, or dolichos, is estimated as having been twenty-four times around the course, or approximately three miles. These three races seemed to have been more or less standardized.

In addition to these three purely athletic events, the races in armor were introduced near the close of the sixth century. These were obviously for military training. Then the Greeks

THE PLAIN OF OLYMPIA

Nestling amid the mountains of Elis is this valley of surpassing beauty where the ancient Olympic games were held. The Alpheus river can be seen at the right and the Hill of Cronus at the left center.

evidently had various relay races, scenes of which are depicted on several vases of that period. The race program also
included events of a ceremonial nature, such as the torch
race.

There is a popular idea that the Greeks held the stadion,
or short race, in pre-eminence over the other events of the
Olympic games, but there seems to be little or no evidence
to support such a contention. The mistaken belief is probably based upon the fact that after the third century B.C.,
each Olympiad was named after the winner of the stadion
sprint and his name entered upon the register.

This great register was originally compiled by Hippias of
Elis. Aristotle and other writers revised and kept it up-to-
date. But recently discovered evidence reveals that the register, prior to the third century B.C., contained the names of
victors in other events. At least we know that writing was
in use at Olympia as early as the seventh century B.C.,
through the official proclamation of the Eleans enforcing the
sacred truce during the period of the games and by the discus
which was long used at Olympia and which bore the name
of Iphitus.

Further doubt upon the first importance of the stadion
race may be seen in the writings of Pindar, who in twenty-
five athletic odes, honors six victors of the stadion and nineteen for various other events. Also we find that out of the
hundred and sixty-three statues in the Altis erected to winners, forty-five were victors in the foot races, twenty for the
pancratium, thirty-nine for wrestling and fifty-nine for
boxing.[1]

The signal for starting the foot races was given, not as
one would suppose, by a judge, but by a herald shouting the
word "Go." Those contestants who tried to obtain an unfair
advantage by jumping the signal were severely lashed and
penalized a yard or two. So the practice was seldom in-
dulged. The starting position seems to be somewhat cramped
and totally at variance with the modern crouch. Various
vases show the starting position of races as having either the

[1] Hyde—De Olympionicarum Statuis

right or left foot a few inches ahead of the other and with
the knees slightly bent and the body leaning forward.

The starting sills at Olympia provided room for twenty
contestants so it seems obvious that many were entered in
the races making necessary the running of several heats. This
was particularly true of the sprints.

The torch races were popular all over Greece. They
consisted of two kinds, a race between individuals and between relay teams. These spectacular races were, of course,
staged at night, the winner being the one who first covered
the course with his torch still afire.

We know little of the training methods employed by the
ancient Grecian athletes. But it is recorded that the runners
ran in deep sand to obtain endurance. They also annointed
their bodies with oil for the actual competition. The Olympic
gymnasium was equipped with a training course of the same
length as the one in the stadium where the athletes could
practice starting and turning the post for the longer races.
Waddling on the knees was also used as a training measure,
a fact mentioned by Aristotle[1]. Epictetus also speaks of regulations governing the athletes diet but gives no particulars[2].

Due to the popularity of the Discobolus of Myron the
discus is more readily associated with the ancient Olympic
games than any other event. To the Greeks, however, it
seems to have been of minor importance as compared with
running, wrestling, boxing and throwing the javelin. To
their practical minds the latter events were of prime importance because they served as a direct training for warfare.

The Homeric poems speak frequently of the discus
throw, but it seems to have been more on the order of hurl-
ing medium-sized rocks or lumps of unwrought iron. The
discus throw apparently was not introduced at Olympia until
about the fifth century.

The Grecian discus was not standardized as to size,
weight or material. Many marble disci are today in museums
but they are too fragile to have been used in the throw.

---

[1] De Gressu   [2] Arrian, iii. 22

Some are inscribed with the names of gods and national heroes. These seem to have been used as religious offerings. Of the fifteen metal disci which have been preserved, eight were recovered at Olympia. The latter range in weight from 1.268 to 5.707 kilograms (three to twelve and a half pounds) and in diameter from about seven to thirteen inches. This variance may be explained by the fact that the lightest ones were used by the boy athletes, while the heaviest ones were used in the pentathlon.

The Grecian method of throwing the discus is problematical for the information on the subject is meager. What we do know is based primarily upon the position of Myron's Discobolus which many modern athletic experts contend is unnatural. Philostratus[1] in describing the accidental killing of Hyacinthus by Apollo with a discus, describes the place from which the discus was thrown (balbis) and the method of throwing as follows: "The balbis is small and sufficient for one man, marked off except behind, and it supports the right leg, the front part of the body leaning forward while it takes the weight off the other leg which is to be swung forward and follow through with the right hand. The thrower is to bend his head to the right and stoop so as to catch a glimpse of his right side, and to throw the discus with a rope-like pull, and putting all the force of the right side into the throw."

Judging from this we must assume that the Grecian discus thrower could run forward to the throwing line before releasing the discus. This method is in sharp contrast to the modern style which is an adaptation of the hammer throw in which the athlete whirls his body around two or three times before releasing the discus.

It is almost impossible to compare the prowess of Grecian discus throwers with those of today due to the scarcity of ancient records and the variance in weight and size between the ancient and the modern disci. It is recorded that Phayllus threw the discus ninety-five Olympic feet, or approximately one hundred English feet, which is about the only ancient

[1] Eranos Vindob, *Juthner*

record we have of this event. The modern discus weighs four pounds and six and fifty-five hundredths ounces and the world's record heave is one hundred and sixty-three feet, eight and three-fourths inches.

The javelin-throwing event of ancient Olympia seems to have been of two kinds, for distance and for accuracy. Up until the close of the fifth century B.C., the throw apparently was for distance as the javelin used was simply a wooden pole or rod of approximately six feet in length and one-half inch in diameter. It was blunt at both ends and very light.

It was thrown from a balbis similar or identical with the one used for the discus throw. This throw was entirely for distance. The ancient Greek used much the same form as the modern javelin thrower in that he ran with the pole to the starting line, drawing back his right hand which held the spear and turning his body sideways and extending his left arm forwards to maintain his balance.

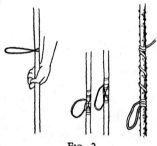

FIG. 2

These drawings show the various methods of attaching the amentum to the javelin shaft. The Greeks used the amentum to give the javelin a rotary motion when thrown which increased the distance and accuracy.

The importance of the javelin as a weapon for light-armed troops caused a change in the javelin throw at Olympia at the close of the fifth century B.C., and the blunt pole was replaced by an actual spear. The purpose of this event then became accuracy, rather than distance, the object being to hit a mark or target. The spear was thrown by contestants both on foot and on horseback.

In throwing both the pole and spear the ancient Greeks used a leather thong, called an amentum, which was fastened near the center of the javelin. They threw it both under and overhanded. This thong, which was from twelve to eighteen inches long, gave the javelin a rotary motion when thrown and greatly increased the distance and accuracy of the throw. It seems to have been detachable and was tightly bound around the shaft leaving a loop large enough for one or two fingers of the thrower's hand. (Fig. 2). No records of distance of ancient javelin throwers have been preserved so we are in the dark as far as knowing what they could do.

Wrestling was one of the most popular sports of ancient Hellas. In point of fact, it is probably the oldest and most universal of all sports. References of wrestling appear time upon time in Grecian literature and wrestling scenes are plentifully depicted upon Grecian coins and vases.

To the ancient Greek wrestling was at once an art and a science. To them it expressed the ideal of ignorance and brute force being conquered by civilization. According to Pindar,[1] Athena taught wrestling to Theseus, who was known as the father of scientific wrestling. In their wrestling contests the Greeks revealed their innate love of skill and gracefulness, for it was not enough to throw an opponent, the job must be done with deftness and finessé. While roughness and brutality were not prohibited they were frowned upon and hence, seldom used. As a matter of fact, wrestling was a part of every Grecian boy's education. He who could not take care of himself in a rough and tumble was looked upon as a weakling.

Two types of wrestling were used by Grecian athletes, "upright" and "ground." The object of upright wrestling was to throw the opponent to the ground and in the event both contestants fell to the ground the match was automatically finished. The upright wrestling style was used in wrestling matches proper and in the pentathlon.

Ground wrestling was used only in connection with the pancratium, a combination of boxing and wrestling. Biting and kicking were allowed in this event and the contest continued until one contestant admitted defeat.

---

[1] Pindar, *Nemean* v 49

At Olympia practice for the wrestling matches were held in the palæstra, which is a Grecian word meaning wrestling-school. Lucian[1] records that the two styles of wrestling were assigned different training locations. Ground wrestling was staged under cover on a spot which had been watered until extremely muddy, which was calculated to make the contest less dangerous, while the mud was thought to be beneficial to the skin. Upright wrestling matches were held in a pit which had been spaded up to form a soft surface, to which sand was often added. The victor had to win three falls. Practically all of the so-called modern holds, except tricky variations, were used by the ancient Greeks.

The contestants at Olympia were drawn by lot for each round and, of course, in the event of there being an odd number, one of them drew a bye. As there were usually around a dozen competitors and the matches continued until one was the undisputed victor, the wrestler drawing a bye had a considerable advantage in the next round when he met a contestant already more or less exhausted. Hence, the luck of the draw could and sometimes did help the ultimate victor. According to Pindar[2] Alcimidas and his brother lost two Olympic crowns by ill luck in the draw. But the Greeks accorded the greater honor to the wrestler who won the crown without having drawn a bye.

---

[1] Lucian, Anacharsis   [2] Pindar, 6th Nemean ode

GRECIAN BOY WRESTLER

An early B. C. Grecian bronze of an Olympic boy wrestler. It is erroneously known as Diskobolus having been
named by someone unacquainted with Grecian athletics who
apparently thought the stance was indicative of a discus
thrower. This statue is one of a pair that was excavated
from a ruined villa in Herculaneum in 1754, and is now in
the Museum of Naples.

A GRECIAN GIRL RUNNER

This early fifth century B.C. statue strikingly portrays the harmonious
development of beauty and athletic prowess of Grecian womanhood.
The original, partially restored, is in the Vatican at Rome.

Chapter IV

ANCIENT OLYMPIC EVENTS (Continued)

> The shepard, and the ploughman, the fowler,
> and he whom the sea feedeth strive but to keep
> fierce famine from their bellies; but whoso in the
> games or in war hath won delightful fame, re-
> ceiveth the highest of rewards in fair words of
> citizens and of strangers.
>
> Pindar, *Isthmian*, i.47 *ff*.

BOXING WAS AS popular as wrestling in ancient Greece. The hero-gods, such as Apollo, Heracles, Ares and others, are pictured in Grecian mythology as boxers of consummate ability. As in wrestling, it was the skill and gracefulness displayed by boxers that appealed to the Hellenes. They also attributed the science of boxing to Theseus. Many scenes of boxing contests are painted on the heroic canvasses of the *Iliad* and the *Odyssey*.

Boxing as a sport originated, of course, in the primitive fight with bare fists. As the sport emerges into recorded history in Greece, however, we find the boxers covering their hands with long, thin leather thongs, which left the thumbs free, known as cæstus. These thongs, while they were not boxing gloves, may as well be so called, were approxi-mately twelve feet long. They were usually cut from cow-hide and were oiled so as to be pliable. Their use was evi-dently not intended so much to deaden the blow or protect the face of an opponent as to protect the knuckles and to add to the force of the blow. The modern boxing glove serves the same purpose.

This method of binding the hands must have been bother-some, to say the least, but its use persisted during the early history of the games, in fact, until early in the fourth cen-tury B.C. Various methods of wrapping the cæstus may be studied in the drawings on pages 48 and 70. These cæstus while they show the Grecian style of binding, are studded with metal knobs, a barbarous Roman invention which made of boxing under their influence a brutal and deadly sport devoid of all science. Be it said to the eternal credit of the Greeks that such cæstus were not used in Grecian boxing matches.

In the fourth century B.C., a boxing glove constructed of some soft material appeared which left the fingers free and extended up the arm almost to the elbow. This boxing glove was made tight by crisscrossing leather thongs which were then tied at the back of the hand. This style was followed by a less cumbersome glove which could be drawn on and off without the bother of tying thongs. It somewhat resembled a fingerless mitt.

The Grecian rules for boxing were extremely simple. There was no ring as the modern world knows it. At Olympia the boxing contests took place either in the palæstra or stadium, which afforded the contestants ample room to advance or retreat and made it practically impossible to corner an opponent. There were no rounds, the boxers fought on until exhausted or one held up his hand in token of surrender. Nor was there any classification according to weight. Regardless of weight the boxing contests were open to all. Hence the heavy boxers enjoyed an advantage unknown today. Clinching and wrestling were not permitted, according to Plutarch[1].

To the Greeks boxing was almost entirely a science of defense. Indeed, we read that in the boxing contests of the Olympic games the boxer who came out of the bout unmarked and who had been able to wear down his opponent by sheer cleverness was regarded with the greater admiration. This defense style was employed largely in the pancratium. For some unknown reason the Greeks did not use body blows. There is no record of a rule to that effect so it may have been an unwritten law.

As in modern boxing, the right to the chin was the "knockout drops" with Grecian boxers. They also seemed to

---

[1] Plutarch. *Symp.* ii.4

have employed the left hook to good advantage. In foot-work, Grecian boxers were unexcelled. Ancient writers often refer to this fact. Statius[1], in describing how Alcidamas defeated his heavier opponent, Capaneus, says, "He (Alci-damas) avoids a thousand deaths which flit around his temples, by quick movement and by the help of his feet."

We can well imagine the Grecian boxer as being extreme-ly agile, using both hands with considerable freedom and employing deft footwork. Of the rules governing boxing contests at Olympia, we know little except what has already been pointed out. As in wrestling the opponents for each round were chosen by lot, a method favoring the contestant who drew a bye. But his advantage did him little good for, having won because of the luck of the draw, his victory was belittled by the spectators.

The primitive rough and tumble fight or "rough-house," of course, was the origin of the Grecian pancratium (Grecian word meaning a complete contest), which was a combination of wrestling and boxing. It was but natural that the active-minded Greeks, having made a science of both wrestling and boxing, would experiment with a combination of the two. That the result was extremely popular in ancient Greece is attested by the many references to it in her literature and scenes of pancratium contests on vases.

One might well believe that such a meleé could be nothing except extremely brutal yet, under the strict rules of the Hellanodicæ at Olympia, it was in fact a contest of skill and strength, although obviously no enterprise for the weakling.

Grecian mythology ascribes its origin to the two patron saints of athletic science and skill, Theseus and Heracles, the former having used the pancratium against the Minotaur and the latter the same art against the Nemean lion. Philostra-tus[2] wrote that the pancratium was the fairest of all athletic contests while Pindar rises to poetical heights in his eight odes in praise of pancratiasts. While it is recorded that

---

[1] Statius, Theb. vi.731   [2] Philostratus, Im ii.6

a few contestants lost their lives while engaged in this lusty contest still the Greeks considered boxing more dangerous.

In the pancratium everything was fair except eye-gouging and biting, which were prohibited by Olympic rules, according to Aristophanes[1]. An official with a rod, which he did not hesitate to wield mightily, stood over the contestants insuring fair play. Hitting, kicking and wrestling were the accepted means of conquering an opponent although strangulation was not unknown.

The hands of the pancratiasts were not wrapped with leather thongs, hence, they could hit both with the open hand and fist. Whether the contest developed along the lines of boxing or wrestling depended, of course, upon the contestants. The one who was more proficient in boxing naturally would endeavor to keep the match within his specialty and vice versa. As a rule the contest was decided on the ground where the stronger wrestler would have the advantage due to the fact that effective hitting would be more or less difficult in that position.

While either hitting or wrestling comprised the majority of the activities of the pancratiasts, kicking also was largely used. The favorite target for the kick was the stomach, a blow that would be disastrous to anyone unless as well protected around the stomach with muscles as were the Greeks. The contest was continued until one or the other was rendered helpless or held up his hand as a signal of defeat.

Jumping as an individual event was not practiced at Olympia, it was a part of the pentathlon only. The Greeks did not jump for height. Grecian jumping seems to have been for distance only and to have consisted of two kinds, standing and running. Their running broad jump would appear to have been more like the modern hop, step and jump than the running broad jump for the only Olympic jumping record that has come down to posterity was one made by Phayllus of Croton who was reputed to have made a leap of fifty-five feet. On the face of it, such a record either has been exaggerated or else it represents a series of jumps.

---

[1] Aristophanes, *Aves*, 442

Jumping events were unknown at Olympia until the pentathlon was introduced in 708 B.C. Pindar does not include it in the list of sports introduced by Heracles at Olympia, nor does he dedicate any of his numerous athletic odes to an Olympic jumper.

Despite this, the jump seems to have been quite popular among Grecian athletes which may be explained by the importance of the weights used in jumping and which played no little part in all branches of physical training.

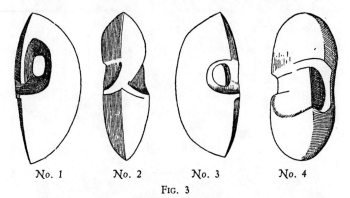

No. 1   No. 2   No. 3   No. 4

FIG. 3

Numbers 1, 2 and 3 are views of a stone halter found at Corinth. Its measurements are approximately 10¼ inches long, 4 inches thick and 3 inches broad. It is cut to form a secure grip for the hand. Number 4 is a stone halter found at Olympia. It weighs over 10 pounds and is 11½ inches long. It apparently antedates the Corinth halter for it is clumsy in comparison with the former.

These jumping weights (Fig. 3) were considerably like the modern dumbbells. The Greeks called them halteres. They varied a deal in shape, size and weight and were made of either stone or metal. They were in use at Olympia as early as the sixth century B.C. The method of using the halteres employed by the Greeks is a natural one, instinctive with any one who uses weights for jumping. The halteres were also generally used for exercise in much the same way as dumbbells are used today.

Here we see how the ancient professional boxers of Greece and Rome engaged in fisticuffs. The metal-studded cæstus indicate they are of about the second century A. D., for Grecian athletes did not employ these forerunners of "brass-knuckles" until the games fell under the baneful influence of Rome.

ΧΥΣΤΟΣ

ANCIENT PUGILISTS

[42]

In most instances a flute was played while the jumper swung the weights backwards and forwards preliminary to the actual jump. This was done evidently under the theory that the rhythm of music would aid the gracefulness and rhythm of the preliminary motions of the jump. Flute music was also used at times to accompany the discus throw and other events.

As is the practice in modern athletics, the Greeks jumped into a pit wherein the ground had been broken up to afford an easy landing. This pit was called a skamma by the Greeks and it seems to have been also used for wrestling. The pit was leveled off so that the imprint of the jumper's feet was easily seen. Philostratus' records that if a jumper stumbled, fell backwards or landed with one foot in advance of the other the jump was not allowed. In other words, the jump must be clean and the landing must be squarely on both feet.

A legend is told about Phayllus of Croton, who having jumped five feet beyond the skamma, broke his leg by landing on the hard ground. Inasmuch as the skamma was supposed to have been fifty feet from the bater or take-off, this would have made his jump fifty-five feet. To cover that distance in one leap seems physically impossible but if, as it seems most likely, the jump really was a hop, step and jump, it is not beyond the bounds of accomplishment, particularly with the help of the halteres.

The pentathlon to the Greeks was the outstanding athletic event contested at Olympia. It consisted of five events, running the stadion, or short foot-race, jumping, throwing the javelin, throwing the discus, and wrestling. It was first introduced in the ancient Olympic games in 708 B.C. We can be positive that these five events comprised the pentathlon through the many references to them by Philostratus in his *Gymnastike*.

Three of these events, each requiring supplementary apparatus, jumping and throwing the javelin and discus were peculiar to the pentathlon alone, and were not held as individual events.

---

[1] Philostratus, *Gymnastike*, 55

These events, together with running and wrestling, epi-
tomized Grecian physical development. The Greeks thought
more of an all-round development than of a specialized one.
Aristotle[1] in his writings highly commends the harmonious development of the pentathlete that produces physical perfection in a glorious combination of strength and gracefulness.
While the pentathlete was inferior to the athlete who specialized in one event yet he was usually vastly superior to
him in all-round ability. This is why the pentathlon was so
popular with the Greeks.

The events of the pentathlon were undoubtedly held in
some fixed order. While we cannot be sure as to just what
that order was, we can at least assume that the wrestling
came last. It would not be logical to expect athletes to perform in the other events at good advantage after a contest as
gruelling as wrestling.

The wrestling in the pentathlon was of the upright variety and three falls were necessary for the victory. The
javelin and discus throw were for distance and the jump was
probably the hop, step and jump.

A great hullabaloo has arisen among Grecian scholars as
to the method used in determining the winner of the pentathlon and many possible systems have been evolved. But
according to the most reliable sources of information including Xenophane[2], the contestant winning three events was
recognized as the victor. In the event that no contestant won
three events then the one holding the most firsts plus the most
seconds and so on was adjudged the winner. At least we are
sure that only those who had won at least one of the other
four events qualified for the last event, wrestling, and that
no pentathlete could be the ultimate victor without having
won at least one event. There appears to be no record of a
bye in the pentathlon, the possibility of which the Greeks
probably avoided by limiting the number of contestants.

When the ancient Hellenes surged southwards from
Central Europe into the Balkan peninsula they had already
domesticated the horse. So it is not surprising to find horse

---

[1] Aristotle, *Rhet.* 1.5   [2] Xenophane, *Hellen.vii.* 4.29

and chariot races playing a large part in their athletic festivals. Chariot racing was added to the Olympic games in
680 B.C., and races for ridden horses in 648 B.C.

The Olympic hippodrome was one of the largest, if not
the largest, in Greece. It lay to the south of the stadium
and near the Alpheus river. While we know its location no
trace of it remains. It was long ago washed away by floods.

The race track, according to the best authorities, of the
Olympic hippodrome was 1538.16 meters (approximately
one mile) in length, although it seems the actual distance
covered by the horses from the aphesis, or starting place,
around the pillar and back was only 1153.62 meters, or approximately three-quarters of a mile.

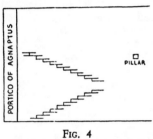

FIG. 4

A sketch (after Weniger) of
the aphesis, or starting device for
the chariot races at Olympia. The
starting line was parallel with
the pillar.

A peculiar and spectacular
starting device (Fig. 4) for
chariot races was used at
Olympia. It was said to have
been devised in the fifth century B.C., by the artist,
Clecetas, and later improved
upon by Aristides.

This starting gate consisted of a series of individual
stalls constructed as a whole
in the shape of a triangle
with the apex towards the
race track and the base at the
Agnaptus portico. Each pair
of stalls (one on each side of
the triangle) were equidistant from the base. To start the
race the ropes in front of the pair of opposite stalls at the
base were withdrawn and as the starting chariots reached a
position even with the next pair of stalls, their ropes were
withdrawn, precipitating two more chariots into the race and
so on down to the last two stalls at the apex. It is not known
exactly how many stalls were provided but Pindar describes
the victory of Arcesilas' chariot over a field of forty entries
at Olympia, which is not unbelievable because of the gener-
ous proportions of the hippodrome. Starting positions were

chosen by lot and of course, due to the character of the starting device, they were always of an even number.

This starting gate, while assuring a fair start for the
chariot races, could not have been any more fair than with
all the entires starting from a single line. It seems to have
been used chiefly because of its dramatic possibilities. While
it was famous all over Greece it was not used elsewhere.

The horse-racing events were added to the Olympic program from time to time and at one time consisted of six
events. Three of these were for horses and three for colts, a
four-horse and two-horse chariot-race and a ridden horse
race. The events for horses were first contested from the
earliest Olympiads while those for colts were added to the
program in the fourth century B.C. A mule chariot-race and
a race for mares were introduced in 500 B.C. A sort of
medley event in which the race was completed by the rider
who had dismounted, was introduced in 496 B.C. The last
three events failed to become popular, however, and were
discontinued in 444 B.C.

According to Pindar[1] the four-horse chariot-race was
twelve times (approximately nine miles) around the hippodrome trace; the two-horse chariot race and the four-colt
chariot race, eight laps; the two-colt chariot race, three laps
and the ridden horse, once around the course. A pillar of
rock marked the turning point and it was here that the
chariots came to the most grief.

The chariot used in the four-horse race was modeled after
the war chariot of antiquity, in which the driver stood up.
The one used in the two-horse race, however, was more of
a cart-like vehicle, which had a seat for the driver. The
jockeys rode without saddles in the horse races.

In most cases drivers and jockeys were paid for their
work and seldom do we find that the owners rode or drove
their own horses. Chariot racing was truly the sport of kings
at Olympia, as only the rich could afford to enter. It was the
dramatic finale of the Olympic games, colorful, spectacular,
exciting and dangerous, often ending in disaster and death.

---

[1] Pindar, *Olympian* 11.50,111 33, vi.75

In the *Electra* of Sophocles, we find a thrilling account of a chariot-race that is well worth reading.

Other events, such a weight lifting, tumbling and tug-of-war, appear at times in the program of events contested at Olympia but they were not popular enough to become a permanent part of the festival.

As in America where we see boys of all sizes emulating the athletic activities of their elders by playing football, baseball, running and jumping in back yards and on sandlots, it was only natural that Grecian boys, attracted by the glamour of the Olympiads, would want to participate. This they were allowed to do and in 616 B.C., we find running, wrestling and boxing contests being held for boys. Boys' events were an integral part of the games for several centuries.

OLYMPIA TODAY

The ruins of once glorious Olympia which gave to the world the rational ideal of "a sound mind in a sound body," (*Mens sana in corpore sano—Juvenal*). The view is looking northwest from the southern wall of the Altis. The foundations of the temple of Zeus are in the foreground. In the background are the museums that house the Hermes of Praxiteles and other art treasures discovered by the German excavators.

CÆSTVS

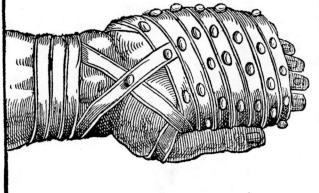

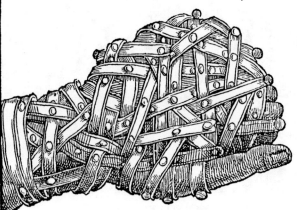

When the ancient Olympic games became professional in character the boxers taped their hands with leather thongs studded with metal, as shown above, making the cæstus a dandy device for massaging the face, a favorite occupation of the Romans

CAESTUS

Chapter V

GOLDEN AGE OF OLYMPIA

> Best of all is water and gold as a flaming fire
> ∙n the night shineth eminent amid lordly wealth;
> but if of prizes in the games thou art fain, O
> my soul, to tell, then as for no bright star more
> quickening than the sun must thou search in the
> void firmament by day, so neither shall we find
> any games greater than the Olympic whereof we
> utter our voice.—*Pindar, Ol.i. (E. Myers' trans-*
> *lation)*.

THE OLYMPIC games during their Golden Age (the fifth
century B. C.) were an expression of the rugged honesty and
sense of fair play of the ancient Greeks, a flowering of the
most priceless athletic ideal the world has ever known. They
flourished during the heyday of manly, artistic and intellectual Greece and resulted from a unique chain of circumstances.

The Grecian victory over the Persians had knit the usually warring tribes of Hellenes into a Panhellenic whole. It
was their first test against an invader and they largely attributed their victory to their athletic prowess. This was but
natural when they compared their own manly soldiers with
the weak and effeminate bodies of their fallen foes.

Hence there ensued a glorification of the athletic ideal in
art and poetry. The Greek ideal became a "sound mind in a
healthy body." All-round development of the mind and
body was their ambition. With their keen eye for beauty
and skill in physical and mental activities, they felt that
weakness and flabbiness of either body or intellect was a
disgrace.

During this Golden Age, Phidias, Myron and Polycletus
were creating marvelous statues of gods and athletes while
Pindar of Thebe and Simonides of Ceos and his nephew,
Bacchylides, were writing their immortal odes to athletic

[49]

heroes. Both art and literature expressed the ideal of the harmonious development of mind and body that was the aim of Grecian education of that period.

Nowhere do we find a more explicit description of this ideal than in Pindar's[1] ode in honor of the victor Agesidamus of Epizephyrian Locri in the boys' boxing contest, Olympiad 76. Listen to the great poet. "If one be born with excellent gifts, then may another who sharpeneth his natural edge, speed him, God helping, to an exceeding weight of glory. Without toil there have triumphed a very few." In other words, he says that those with natural ability must work and train under competent teachers in order to make the best all-round development of their talents. Thus dignity was added to athletes who counted not the toil and hardships of training because it was undertaken for no selfish purpose or gain but for fame. And victory brought honor not only to the winner but also to his city and family.

Pindar's[2] writings also reveal the Greeks' love of the spice of danger in their sports. "Deeds of no risks are honorless whether done among men or among hollow ships," is one of his glowing verses. The Grecian athletes were men of "unbending spirit," courageous, not adverse to much training, for as Phytheas wrote, "practice perfects the deed," and worked for not only strength but also for skill and gracefulness, all being directed by a calm and intelligent brain. This athletic ideal was so virile that it has lived down through the ages.

The Greeks loved beauty and gracefulness in all facets of life, be it poetry, literature, sculpture, architecture, music or athletics. To them athletics were poetry in motion while their statues were frozen athletic poetry.

Not the mere winning of an event was the notable thing with the Greeks. Rather the skill, the gracefulness, and the intelligence displayed by the contestant were the criteria of the champion. Athletics were their means of expressing poetry in terms of action.

Pride in accomplishment was a pertinent index to the Grecian character. Lycurgus is said by Plutarch to have had

---

[1] Pindar, *Olympian*, xi   [2] Pindar, *Olympian* vi 9

always near him someone who had been an Olympic victor.
He relates an anecdote of a Lacedæmonian who was hard put
to throw his antagonist. One of the spectators asked him,
"And now, Sir Lacedæmonian, what are you the better for
your victory?" He answered, smiling, "I shall fight next
the king "

Too, the Greeks had an innate sense of the fitness of
things. Plutarch records an illuminating incident that reveals
this characteristic. Themistocles, who was said to have been
base-born, displeased the Greeks because he came to the
Olympic games in a lavish equipage. There he staged expen-
sive entertainments in richly furnished tents. This magnifi-
cence, the Greeks reasoned, might be allowed the son of a
great family "but was a great piece of insolence in one as yet
undistinguished, and without title or means for making such
a display."

Singleness of purpose also characterized the ancient
Greeks. "Sport for sport's sake" well could have been their
motto. This characteristic is seen in other phases of Grecian
life and activities. The Greek drama carried but a single
story. A story within a story was unknown. Irrelevant sub-
jects did not arise in their plays. Grecian temples were built
solely as habitations for their gods and as a store place for
the valuable gifts offered to them by worshippers, and no
kind of architecture or ornamentation distracted from this
idea. Simplicity and clarity distinguished Grecian activities.
To them the useful unadorned was beautiful.

But this very glorification of the Grecian ideal which
tended towards exaggeration sowed the seeds of specialization in sports which in turn opened the doors to professionalism and ultimately brought about the decline of the Olympic
games as far as their original purpose was concerned. In
their adulation of athletic prowess the Greeks caused the
athletes to overlook a harmonious development and to spe-
cialize on one event. All-round ability for the love of sport
was superseded by a burning desire to become the champion.
Here is where sport for sport's sake disappeared and professionalism began to creep in. Yet this development cannot

be blamed upon the ideal. It is the fault, rather, of over-emphasis. Indeed, it was the ideal of pure sport, which, even when professionalism was seeping into the games, continued to hold high the prestige of Olympia.

Let us, in our imagination, visit an Olympiad of the Golden Age. Early in the fall preceding the year of the games the Eleans, who had charge of Olympia during the greater part of its existence, sent envoys to all Grecian cities and states throughout the known world inviting them to designate contestants for the forthcoming Olympiad. The chosen athletes then went into training in their home cities for a period of nine months. The last month of the training period was required to be spent in Elis.

Approximately two months before the games envoys (known as the truce-bearers of Zeus) were again sent out from Elis. Bearing herald's staves in their hands and wearing wreaths of olive leaves they proclaimed a holy truce through-out Greece for the period of the games. No one bearing arms could enter sacred Olympia. Contestants and the great army of spectators were declared to be under the special protection of Zeus and were immune from molestation by highwaymen, armies and rulers.

This truce, while purely localized to Olympia and possibly of a month's duration at first, made such a deep impression upon the Greeks that it soon was observed all over the Grecian world and was lengthened to three months, allowing ample time for the pilgrimage to and from Olympia.

This is a most striking example of the sporting characteris-tics of the ancient Greeks. No matter if wars were being waged by any or all of the cities and states this general truce was respected by unanimous consent during which the busi-ness of legalized murder was put aside in a nation-wide observance of the Olympiad.

City might be arrayed against city, or state against state, yet when time for the Olympic games rolled around all con-troveries were laid aside. The Greeks had, more than any race that has existed, the saving grace of not taking them-selves or their affairs too seriously.

Everyone might travel openly and without fear. Bandits forsook their trade and even criminals were unmolested, while debtors were granted immunity. It was a period of true freedom and probably the only period of time in the entire history of the world that man went about his business knowing that no one would harm him or interfere with his peaceful activities and he, in grateful recognition of the security vouchsafed, felt it unsportsmanlike to molest any of his fellows.

Violators of the truce were dealt with summarily and forced to pay a heavy fine to the Olympian Zeus. The truce was generally lived up to. Alexander the Great saw fit to make restitution and apologies to an Athenian who, on his way to Olympia, had been set upon and robbed by a band of his soldiers.[1] And even Sparta felt the sting of rebuke for an infraction of this custom when, during the Peloponnesian war, her armed forces entered Olympia during the period of the truce. She was heavily fined and excommunicated and her athletes denied the privilege of entering the games.

The truce bearers of Zeus invited all Grecian freemen (slaves were not permitted to view the games) and citizens to come to Olympia for the games.

And come they did!

Beginning with the period of truce visitors began to pour into Olympia. They came from every section of Greece and from Syracuse, Crete, Marseilles and other far-flung Grecian colonies.

Richly-robed merchants, princes, mendicants, darkly colored men from the hot shores of Africa, flaxen-haired nomads of the barbarous northern lands rubbed elbows with poets, sculptors, musicians, historians, philosophers, statesmen and soldiers. Were they not all Greeks, and despite their petty wars and misunderstandings, were they not all to do honor to Zeus and participate in the great festival?

They came on foot and mule-back, in richly appointed caravans and in picturesque Mediterranean barques that sailed up the Alpheus river to Olympia.

---

[1] Thucydides v.49

It was a great school of learning for all. Men sat at the feet of philosophers, historians and poets. They listened to musicians. A general air of culture pervaded the festival. Merchants displayed their wares and hucksters did a lively business in drinks and foodstuffs.

Olympia was not a town. It was a shrine. Outside of the temples and gymnasia there were no buildings. Those who could afford it brought tents and those who couldn't, slept out under the stars. A great tent city soon arose.

Long-parted friends and acquaintances got together to renew friendships and to tell of their experiences. Affairs of state were broadcast by heralds. Terms of treaties were made known. In short, it was a clearing house of Grecian thought and activities.

Each visitor made his visit to the temple where sat Phidias' marvelous statue of Zeus. The official representatives of cities and states rode in a procession to the temple of Zeus bearing costly gifts.

The festival lasted five days. The first and last day consisted largely of public and private sacrifices and feasts. The middle days, therefore, were left for the sports. The order of the events evidently changed somewhat according to circumstances and conditions but inasmuch as the games were chiefly of a religious nature it is reasonable to suppose that the sacrifices came first, followed by the contests and then the feasts.

There were no seats for spectators. They must take their place on the slopes of the Cronian hill. It was a case of "first-come, first seated." Hours before sunrise the visitors were seeking advantageous positions from where they might witness the games. They brought food and drink with them for to leave for an instant one's place would mean to lose it. There each sat happily all day long, according it an honor to be a unit in that vast and famous assemblage.

Shortly after sunrise the games began. The Hellanodicæ, dressed in purple robes, followed by the contestants, their trainers and the heralds entered the stadium through a special door at the northeast corner of the Altis. A herald then announced the names of all the athletes and asked if there were any charges to be brought against any one of them. Next came an impressive address by some personage or one of the Hellanodicæ.

A thrill of expectancy ran through the poly-glot crowd —the games were about to begin. It had been no little chore for many of these spectators to reach their places on the Cronian hillside. They had come many miles and braved many dangers on land and sea. Can one doubt the strong pull of the Olympic magnet that drew them to this great festival considering the time and money required for travel in those ancient days, and the dangers that beset their pilgrimage?

FIG. 5

Interior of cylix (a two-handled dr nking vessel) showing how an Olympic victor was crowned by one of the Hellanodicæ. The garlands and palms showered upon the winner are also in evidence. This cylix is now in the Bibliotheque Nationale of Paris.

Before each event the herald proclaimed the names of the entries, their fathers' names, and their home cities. After each event the winner was showered with flowers and garlands by the specta-tors and immediately crowned with the olive wreath by one of the Hellanodicæ. In Fig. 5 we see depicted such a scene which was taken from the interior of a cylix (a two-handled drinking cup used by the Greeks) now in Bibli-otheque Nationale. In case of a tie the crown was of-fered to some god.

In the first six ancient Olympiads the prizes were usually articles of value such as tripods. Prior to the sev-enth Olympiad (752 B. C.) the Delpic oracle was said to have advised that a crown of the sacred wild olive leaves in the Altis be given the victor. This, then, became the custom.

A golden sickle, wielded by a boy of pure Grecian descent

This old wood cut gives us an idea of the wonderful physical development of the ancient Grecian athletes. The presence of the two bald-headed gentlemen in the back row would indicate that wrestling was enjoyed by all ages.

GRECIAN WRESTLERS

whose parents were both living, was used to cut the branches of the olive tree from which were made the victors' wreaths. From the practice of placing a wreath or laurel upon the heads of victors is derived our modern saying "to win one's laurels."

This was their only reward as far as the games themselves were concerned. Winners, however, were allowed to erect statues of themselves within the sacred confines of the Altis near the temple of Zeus. Most of these statues have vanished but it was here that the German excavators uncovered the Hermes of Praxiteles, a statue which represents the flower of Grecian physical development and the most perfect male form the world has ever seen.

This simple custom was the heart and soul of pure amateurism and it was largely responsible for the lasting benefits of the games. That men should train strenuously for months for an olive wreath rather than for a valuable consideration astonished the ancient world and today is still little understood.

It is recorded that, following the battle of Thermopylæ, the Greeks suspended the war against the Persians in order to celebrate the Olympic games. Xerxes, the Persian king, was much impressed when told that his adversaries had withdrawn to participate in and view the national athletic festival. Greatly interested in this strange behavior he asked concerning the prizes awarded the victors.

"Naught but wreaths of olive leaves," was the reply.

Dumfounded, Xerxes is said to have exclaimed:

"By the Gods, what manner of men are these who contend with one another not for money but for honor!"

When the victors reached their home cities, however, their rewards were more tangible. They were met outside the walls by the entire populace. At the head of an acclaiming procession the victor marched into his native city usually through a fresh breach in the wall. They became persons of no little importance and they were fêted extensively and their praises sung by poets. Many cities, notably Athens, pensioned them for life.

We are not certain of the exact order of events. But the Greeks, being lovers of system and the natural trend of events to a well-defined climax, can be assumed to have staged their great athletic festival along these lines.

The logical order would seem to place the events for boys first followed by the men's foot races, all these probably taking place on the first day of competition.

The second day saw contests in wrestling, boxing and the pancratium, presumably in the order given. On the last day before the final day of sacrifices and feasts came the horse-races, the race in armor and the pentathlon.

What a glorious spectacle it was. Excitement and drama ran riot. There was something doing every minute of the day and night. Small wonder that men were willing to endure hardships and dangers to view one of the greatest festivals ever to be staged in recorded history.

In the evenings the bright Grecian moon looked down upon scenes of splendor and activity as processions of exulting and rejoicing friends followed their favorite victors about the Altis to the accompaniment of flute music Archilochus' old hymn of victory[1] was sung and perhaps some new song written by Bacchylides or Pindar specially for a new champion. Victors were then entertained at banquets which sometimes lasted the night through. The last day seems to have been almost entirely given over to sacrifices, feasts and revelry.

Through the welter of life's perplexities stabs the golden arrow of the Grecian ideal of play for play's sake, one of life's few unselfish manifestations.

Certainly nowhere in the recorded history of races that lived contemporaneously with the ancient Greeks do we find any evidence of organized sports or play activities.

In Palestine, during the Golden Age of Greece, when the Olympic Games were in their heyday, the Israelite tribes, treacherous and densely ignorant, apparently had no forms of play. According to history their time was chiefly spent in

[1] Pindar. *Olympian. ix.1,2*

wars and in heaping various species of living sacrifices upon altars, which later probably added considerably to the variety of their priests' menu.

Palestine being a poverty-stricken stretch of rock and sand unfit for agricultural pursuits and lying in the natural trade route from east to west, its inhabitants, the Israelites, became of necessity traders and, hence, good bookkeepers. So we find them enumerating at enormous length the list of their burnt offerings and religious ceremonies. The Greeks, on the other hand, were content with the mere statement that "sacrifices were offered."

Other contemporary races, the Persians and Egyptians, paid little or no attention to play. The Persians were steeped in the Oriental mysticism and practices of Western Asia which they had conquered, while the Egyptians were torn and exhausted by an eternal warfare for supremacy between the priests and Pharoahs.

Comparisons may be odious but they are often illuminating. In this case they show us the fundamental differences of the races to which we have referred and why the Olympic games were so revealing of the Grecian character.

Unhampered by the dead hands of tradition the ancient Greeks developed a rational and joyful manner of living. Life to them was a means of expression and they ever sought to perfect that expression, whether it be in the arts or in physical and mental activities.

When Christianity settled down upon the world with its tenets that the body of man was a thing impure and evil the ideal of physical perfection disappeared and with it the ideal of sport for sport's sake. Under this influence the body was subjected to self-inflicted tortures. There was no opportunity for play and the joyful expression of life in mental and physical activities.

So through the Dark Ages sport was taboo. While religious and political wars soaked the earth with blood, men had no time for play. Not until the world reached back into the ages for the precious flower of Grecian civilization did sport again come into its own.

But in our adulation of the ancient Greeks let us not assume a supine position of blind worship. The Hellenes themselves would resent such an attitude. Let us also recognize their faults. But let us at least give them credit for first bringing a rationalistic mode of living into the world and of loving play for its own sake.

We must regard the Greeks as children and as such contemplate Olympia as their national playground. As far as that is concerned, in the light of recorded history, we of this age are also but children for only a short span of some seventy generations separate us from the Hellenes.

OLYMPIC CLOWNING

The ancient Greeks never took themselves very seriously. Above is seen a comic event which was staged at athletic festivals. Old men were dressed, or undressed clownishly, and after a run, they jumped upon a greased wine-skin full of wine. The object was to keep their balance, a practically impossible accomplishment. The resulting antics threw the crowds into gales of Homeric laughter. This print was taken from an original wood engraving which appeared in de Arte Gymnastica in 1672.

CHAPTER VI

WOMEN AND THE OLYMPIC GAMES

> The Grecian female divinities were Hera, the
> proud and jealous queen of Zeus; Athena, who
> sprang full-grown from the forehead of Zeus, the
> goddess of wisdom and domestic arts; Artemis,
> the goddess of the chase; Aphrodite, the goddess
> of love and beauty born of the white sea foam;
> Hestia, the goddess of the hearth and Demeter,
> the earth mother, the goddess of grains and
> harvests. . . . . . The chief gods and goddesses of
> the Greeks, in striking contrast with the mon-
> strous divinities of the oriental mythologies, had
> been moulded by the fine Hellenic imagination
> into human forms of surpassing beauty and grace.
>
> *Anon*

THE WOMEN of ancient Greece were excluded from the
Olympic games, both as spectators and participants.

Their exclusion was not based upon lack of athletic
ability for the Grecian statues and bronzes that have come
down to us reveal a womanhood strong and virile. Such physical perfection and beauty could only result from athletic
prowess.

Various scholists have reasoned that women were not
permitted to view the games because the contestants wore
exactly nothing. This theory, however, must be discarded in
view of the fact that modesty, as the modern world knows
it, meant little or nothing to any ancient race. This fact becomes apparent from a study of tribal customs and habits of
all races of that period.

A theory closer to the truth would be that women were
excluded from the Olympic games because of some religious
taboo peculiar to that festival. Another explanation might
be found in the fact that there were no accommodations for
women at Olympia. We have already read how most of the
spectators slept out under stars. There were no buildings
except the various temples and, of course, these could not be
profaned with the presence of either men or women.

[61]

So it is reasonable to suppose that their exclusion was due to one or the other of the above reasons. Certainly we know that girls and women were not excluded from other Grecian athletic festivals where male contestants performed in the nude.

The women of Ionia were allowed to witness the games at Delos, a condition also true of the Isthmian games which were of a more religious character. In Sparta the girls were trained in athletic pursuits side by side with the boys.

One bit of evidence in support of the religious taboo may be seen in the lone exception of the exclusion of women to the Olympic games. This only known exception was in the case of the Priestess of Demeter Chamyne, who apparently sat as an oracle during the period of the games.

The rule was that no woman could cross the Alpheus river for probably a week before the games, while they were in progress and for a few days following their termination. Death was the penalty of violation. It seemed to be the custom to hurl the culprit from the Typæan rock.

There is recorded only one infraction of this rule. Disguised as a trainer, Pherenice, a member of the illustrious clan of Diagoridæ, anxious to see her son, Peisirodus, perform in one of the boys' boxing matches, seconded him during the fight. Peisirodus won and in her pleasure at his victory, she jumped over the enclosure, thus disclosing her sex.

In consideration of her maternal love and because her father and brothers all had been Olympic victors the Hellanodicæ (Olympic judges) pardoned her. But to provide against a recurrence of this episode they passed a rule that in the future all trainers should appear naked.[1]

While Grecian women were excluded personally from the games, they were permitted to enter their horses in the chariot-races. Many were known to have erected statues in the Altis to commemorate their victories.

Not to be outdone by the men, however, the women instituted their own version of the Olympic games. This festival was held once every four years and followed shortly

---

[1] Pausanias. v.6,7.

after the regular games. It was known as the Heræa[1]. Sixteen women, eight of Elis and eight of Pisa, wove a peplos, a shawl-like garment, for Hera (the wife of Zeus) in whose honor the festival was held.

The contests seemed to have been restricted to races for girls of various age classifications. There were no other events. The length of their races was 500 Grecian feet, or one-sixth less than the men's stadion races.

The attire for the races was picturesque and practical. They wore a high-waisted, short tunic reaching about half way down to the knee and with the right shoulder and breast bare. Their hair was uncaught and streamed down their shoulders. They ran barefooted.

Women victors received the same prize as the men, a wreath of olive leaves from the sacred grove. And in addition they were awarded a share of the heifer which had been sacrificed to Hera prior to the races. Like the men victors, they were allowed to set up their statues in the Altis.

A copy of a statue of a girl runner of the fifth century B.C., is in the Vatican, (Page 36). The leg development attests to her athletic training but unfortunately the arms have been restored. It is thought that the maiden is in a position for the start of the race. According to Greek mythology the women's Olympics of Heræa, were founded by Hippodameia as a celebration of her marriage to Pelops. With the exception of a few instances, recorded history has overlooked the Heræa and these references are so meager as to leave us almost completely ignorant as to its history.

One can, however, imagine the Heræa to have been an athletic institution which contributed largely to the health and beauty of the Grecian women. Here, again, we find that the ancient Greeks originated a movement which had as its motive the development of superior human beings.

It is gratifying that, after long centuries of repression due to false modesty and religious taboos, women are again taking their rightful place in athletics. Their participation in many events of the modern Olympiads means much for the betterment of the human race.

---

[1] Pausanias. v.16.

A study of the above woodcut reveals the fact that the ancient Olympic athletes knew as much about wrestling as we do. Here we see toeholds, head-scissors and what-have-you. The pancratium was a combination of wrestling and boxing, a pastime much beloved by the Greeks.

PANCRATIASTS

[64]

Chapter VII

DECLINE OF ANCIENT GAMES

> Of all the countless evils throughout Hellas
> there is none worse than the race of athletes. In
> youth they strut about in splendour, the pride of
> their city, but when bitter old age comes upon
> them they are cast aside like threadbare gar-
> ments . . . I blame the custom of the Hellenes
> who gather together to watch these men, honor-
> ing a useless pleasure.
>
> Euripides, *Autolycus*

WE HAVE ALREADY seen how the Grecian victory over Persia
fused the warring Hellenic tribes into a Panhellenic nation.
This national unity, abetted by art and literature, preserved
the pure spirit of athletics until the Greeks again fell out
among themselves. When the Peloponnesian war broke out
hero-worship of the athlete had grown to such proportions
that specialization had already set in.

When athletics become an end in themselves their useful
sphere of recreation and exercise in an all-round development ceases. When naught counts but the mere winning of
a contest then specialization appears. Specialization demands
time for training and money for trainers. Close on the heels
of specialization comes professionalism or the business of
sport, which is the antithesis of pure amateurism, or sport for
sport's sake.

So in the fourth century we find athletes going through
their paces under the watchful eyes of trainers. Tisias, who
trained Glaucus of Corystus[1] is the first trainer of whom we
hear although Pindar mentions several later.

---

[1] Philostratus, *Gymnastike*, 20

In the palæstra and gymnasia the Greeks first used trainers for wrestling and boxing. It did not take them long to fathom that special training was of material benefit in athletic contests and that a special diet was an additional aid.

During the Golden Age of Olympia a harmonious development of body and mind had been the Grecian ideal. Now that imperceptibly shifted into one-sided development or specialization. Socrates[1] complains of this change in the national ideal. "The runner has over-developed his legs, and the boxer the upper part of his body," he wrote.

Before athletic specialization set in, Grecian athletes had no special diet. They ate as did the entire population. Their menu consisted of figs, cheese, porridge and meal-cakes. Meat was eaten sparingly, chiefly as a relish.

Here another influence towards specialization is seen. Inasmuch as the Greeks had no weight classifications for wrestling and boxing the heavy contestant generally had the advantage. When it was discovered that by eating meat athletes could add considerably to their weight, they went on a special diet. This set them apart from the ordinary run of men by creating an athletic class.

The time of these athletes was entirely taken up by eating, training and sleeping, leaving no time for intellectual development. This procedure was diametrically opposed to the Grecian ideal of harmonious development. Xenophon[2] wrote that "Socrates disapproved of such a life as incompatible with the cultivation of the mind." While gluttonous eaters were described in the Grecian idiom as "eating like a wrestler."

Moreover these specialized athletes became worthless for aught except athletic contests. They were considered useless as warriors. Plato[3] said of them, "The athlete's nature is sleepy and the least variation from his routine is liable to cause him serious illness," while Euripides wrote, "The athlete is the slave of his jaw and of his belly."

---

[1] Socrates, *Memorabilia* iii, 10,6   [2] Xenophon, *Mem.* i.2,4.   [3] Plato, *Rep.* iii,404

But the great body of Grecian peasants could not perceive where these tendencies were leading and they began to lavish rich rewards upon Olympic victors. The inevitable result was professionalism. The contestants at Olympia were not paid directly for participation but indirectly with purses and gifts following the games.

During the Golden Age of Olympia Hellas had been a nation of athletes. Now we see them no longer athletic. The change was bitterly denounced by Aristophanes[1] who describes the youth of Greece as having become too feeble to run even in a torch-race. The Greeks became a nation of spectators rather than contestants. Athletics at Olympia passed into the hands of professionals or unspoiled boys from the mountainous districts while the rich centered their attention on chariot-racing.

Corruption reared its ugly head at Olympia. Victories were bought and sold. In the Olympiad of 388 B.C., Eupolus[2] of Thessaly bribed his boxing opponents to let him win first place. It was discovered by the Eleans and the culprits were heavily fined. In 332 B.C. Callippus[3] of Athens bribed his adversaries in the pentathlon. Its discovery again drew heavy fines and the Eleans issued a warning that "not with money but with speed of foot and strength of body must prizes be won at Olympia."

The decline of the Olympic games continued over a long period. The growth of professionalism may be discerned in the increasing list of athletes who were victorious in more than one event in the same Olympiad. Among these may be mentioned Leonidas of Rhodes who won all four of the foot-races in three successive Olympiads, 164, 160, and 156 B.C., and Phillinus of Cos, who is credited with having won twenty-four stadion-races at various athletic festivals, three of which were won at Olympia.

Such was the state of affairs at the time of the Roman conquest of Greece. For a century following the fall of Corinth the spirit of the Olympic games was close to extinc-

---

[1] Aristophanes, Nub. 961 [2] Pausanias, v.21,5. [3] Ibid

tion. Sulla transferred the entire festival to Rome in 80 B.C. Only the boys' foot-race was run that year at Olympia. Evidently he planned to hold the festival permanently in Rome but he died before his object would be accomplished.

While the Romans enjoyed exercise of all kinds they did not relish competition. This trait, coupled with the fact that for centuries they had known nothing but warfare, left the uncivilized sons of Remus and Romulus sadly lacking in athletic ideals. Incessant fighting had brutalized them to the point that they cared only for vicious and deadly gladiatorial contests, and they were interested in these only as spectators. They could not understand the Grecian ideal of sport for sport's sake and did not even care to watch Grecian athletic festivals.

Yet so virile was Grecian civilization that the Romans finally became somewhat Hellenized. Greece became the teacher of her conqueror. The Romans, freed of war during this short priod, began to take up festivals of all kinds. Rome, in an attempt to strengthen her position in Greece, gave Olympia the doubtful honor of imperial patronage.

Nero himself entered an Olympiad as a contestant and won, probably through bribery, various events, such as chariot racing and the singing competition. Then, when departing, he carried with him to Rome hundreds of works of art from the Altis. Arriving in Rome he aped the Grecian custom of having an Olympic victor enter his home city through a new breach in the wall. Such actions brought Olympia into even greater contempt in Italy as attested by Seneca and other Roman writers.

While this was going on the Roman participation in the Olympic games had been degrading the athletic taste of the Greeks. An evidence of this is the Roman introduction of the brass-studded cæstus in the boxing matches. These contests then became murderous exhibitions of bloodshed rather than a display of scientific skill.

Degraded and broken, betrayed by friend and foe alike, the ancient Olympic games finally came to the end of the trail. The 292nd Olympiad held in the year 392 A.D., was the final one. It is a paradox that the games, originally started as a religious festival in honor of a Grecian god, were abolished by Emperor Theodosius (394 A.D.) presumably because he thought they were opposed to the tenents of another religion, the Christian.

And so, after 1168 years, the ancient Olympiads came to an end. The list of stadion victors which opened with the name of a Grecian cook, Corœbus of Elis in 776 B.C., closed with the name of an Armenian, Varastad, in 392 A.D.

THE TEMPLE OF HERA

The ruins of the first building erected at Olympia as they appear today. The temple of Hera is thought to be the oldest one in Greece. Hera was the wife of Zeus and the patron saint of the women's Olympic games.

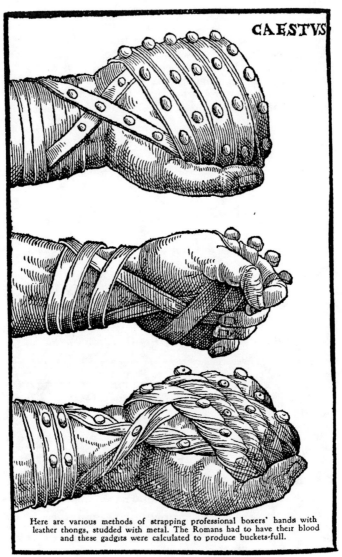

CAESTVS

Here are various methods of strapping professional boxers' hands with leather thongs, studded with metal. The Romans had to have their blood and these gadgits were calculated to produce buckets-full.

METAL-STUDDED CAESTUS

[70]

CHAPTER VIII

MODERN OLYMPIC GAMES

We swear that we will take part in the
Olympic Games in loyal competition, respecting
the regulations which govern them and desirous
of participating in them in the true spirit of
sportsmanship and for the glory of sport.
Oath of contestants in modern Olympiads.

THE GRECIAN ideal of an active mind in a healthy body as
exemplified in the Olympic games lay dormant through the
Dark Ages, through feudalism and through the beginning efforts of mankind to place the world again upon a broadminded basis of tolerance and intellectualism.

Baron Pierre de Coubertin, a Frenchman, is credited with
the modern revival of the Olympic games. In 1894, he wrote
to the heads of various sports organizations throughout the
world suggesting a re-establishment of the Olympiads. He
wrote in part, "Before all things it is necessary that we
should preserve those characteristics of nobility and chivalry
which have distinguished it in the past, so that it may continue to play the same part in the education of the peoples
of today as it played so admirably in the days of ancient
Greece. Imperfect humanity has ever tended to transform
the Olympic athlete into the paid gladiator. But the two
things are incompatible. We must choose between the one
formula and the other."

De Coubertin then travelled to the leading nations telling
them of his plans for the revival of the ancient Grecian
Olympic games. He was warmly received all over the world.
Sweden was first to officially sanction his ideal, and the
United States was second in lending him support.

As a result of his efforts a committee was appointed
which met in Paris, France, in 1895. It was decided to re-

vive the Olympic games. The committee felt that a series of Olympiads, with contestants from all nations competing, would go far in fostering international understanding and peace as well as revive the old Grecian ideal of sportsmanship.

The following year, 1896, the first of the modern series of Olympiads was held, appropriately enough, in Athens, Greece. Due to the generosity and efforts of George Aberhoff, a wealthy Greek, Crown Prince Constantine and the Greek Olympic committee, a magnificent stadium of white marble was erected on the site of the old Athenian stadium.

The marathon race was inaugurated at this Olympiad. It was not an event of the ancient games. The marathon was incorporated in the modern Olympics to commemorate the fête of Pheidippides who, in 490 B.C. ran from Marathon to Athens with the news that the Greeks had defeated the Persians under Darius.

The stadium, although a beautiful thing, was not large enough to contain a suitable running track. Only fourteen events were held and of these the United States won nine; Great Britain, three and Greece and Denmark one each. The American team consisted of only six athletes. Greece was much disappointed because of the failure of her athletes to win events but made much of the victory of a Grecian peasant in the marathon race.

The second Olympiad was held in Paris, France, in 1900. This Olympiad had twenty-two events of which the United States won seventeen; Great Britain, three and France and Hungary one each.

The French people took little or no interest in these games which were held without proper organization and publicity. Many events of a trivial nature were contested, such as fishing in the Seine river. A. G. Spaulding had charge of the American team of fifty-five members. The United States was the only nation well represented in all events.

The scene of the Olympiads shifted to the New World for the first time in 1904 when the third Olympiad was held in St. Louis, Missouri, in connection with an exposition. These games had little world-wide importance, however, because practically all the contestants were Americans. Few Europeans were entered because of the expense. The United States spared no effort to make the games successful but because of the limited entry list they were a failure as far as an international sport festival is concerned.

Due to the abortive games in 1904, the fourth Olympiad was held in 1906, and for the second time in Athens, Greece. This year there were twenty-three events of which the United States won eleven; Great Britain, four; Greece, three; Sweden, two and Germany, Austria and Russia one each.

The fifth Olympiad was held in London in 1908. Other events in addition to track and field contests were added this year, such as shooting matches, swimming, etc. For the first time since the modern revival of the games the United States was not the winner of the athletic festival due largely to the fact that few Americans were entered in the broader scope of events except those of track and field. The point score of all events resulted as follows: Great Britain, one hundred and fifty-five; United States, one hundred and thirty-one; Sweden, thirty-one; Germany, twenty-one and France, fifteen.

The 1908 games were not adequately advertised nor were proper preparations made, yet despite this they drew some 300,000 spectators and 2,647 entries from twenty-two nations.

Stockholm, Sweden, was the location of the sixth Olympiad, held in 1912. Again the United States was not fully represented in the complete list of events with the exception of track and field contests. The point score was: Sweden, one hundred and thirty-three; United States, one hundred and twenty-nine; Great Britain, seventy-six; Finland, fifty-two; Germany, forty-seven; France, thirty-two; Denmark, nineteen; South Africa, Hungary and Norway, sixteen each; Canada, Italy and Australia, thirteen each; Belgium, eleven; Austria and Russia, six each; Greece, four; and Holland, three.

Originally the seventh Olympiad was scheduled to be held in Berlin in 1916, but did not take place because the World War was raging at that time. The Germans made elaborate preparations for the seventh Olympiad. They built a mag- nificent stadium in Berlin and with their usual thoroughness planned to make the games highly successful. Hence, the seventh Olympiad was held four years later, 1920, in Ant- werp, Belgium. International sport, however, was illy pre- pared for the games, coming as they did, so soon after the end of the war and consequently this meet was of negligible importance.

For the second time Paris, France, became the scene of the modern Olympic games, when the eighth Olympiad was held there in 1924. This meet saw the introduction of events for women, including swimming and tennis. It was an Olympiad of true international aspect because of the large number of nations represented. The games began with the winter sports at Chamouix in January and ended with the track and field events at Paris.

Of the twenty-six track and field events the United States won twelve; Finland, nine; Great Britain, three; Austria and Italy, one each. A resumé of all branches of the games shows that the United States won championships in boxing, wrestling, lawn tennis, swimming, rowing, target shooting, Rugby football and track and field events. Norway was first in winter sports, yachting and hunting marksman- ship. France took the fencing and cycling championships. Sweden won the equestrian events and the pentathlon; Fin- land, the Græco-Roman wrestling; Argentine, polo; Uruguay, Association football; Italy, weight-lifting; while Czecho- Slovakia and Switzerland tied in gymnastic events.

A quickened world-wide interest in the Olympic games made the ninth Olympiad, which was held in Amsterdam, Holland, in 1928, the most successful of all the modern meets. A large number of nations were represented and the rivalry of the contestants intense and spirited. The ninth Olympiad saw the establishment of twelve new Olympic records, striking proof of the quality of competition and ability of the athletes.

ΔΙΣΚΟΒΟΛΟΙ·

This ancient pastime appears to be the granddaddy of our so-called modern game of horseshoes. But the Greeks had another name for it—quoit or discus throwing.

GRECIAN QUOIT THROWERS

[75]

The winter sports were held in January at St. Moritz, and the games ended with the track and field events at Amsterdam in July. The United States won nine of the twenty-six track and field contests; Finland, five; Canada, four; Great Britain, two; and Japan, Poland, Germany, France, Sweden and South Africa, one each. The point score in this division for the leaders was: United States, one hundred and seventy-three; Finland, one hundred and two; Great Britain, forty-six; Sweden, forty-four; Germany, forty-four; Canada, thirty-eight; France, twenty-seven; Japan, nineteen and South Africa, fourteen.

The United States won championships this year in but three divisions of the games; viz: swimming, rowing and the track and field events. Sweden won the pentathlon and tied with Finland in wrestling and with France and Norway in yachting. Norway annexed the winter sports; Germany the weight-lifting and Græco-Roman wrestling and tied Holland in horse-racing; France, fencing; Italy, boxing; Denmark, cycling and Switzerland, gymnastics.

Germany won the ninth Olympiad with a total of forty-five and one-half points scored in all divisions of the games. The United States came in second with thirty-nine points followed in order by Holland, thirty-five; Italy, thirty-three and one-half; Finland, thirty; Sweden, twenty-eight and one-half; Great Britain, eighteen and other nations with lesser totals.

Contrary to a popular belief the United States has not been the winner, either officially or unofficially, of all the modern Olympiads. Great Britain won the games in 1908, Sweden in 1912 and Germany in 1928. The United States has won, however, the track and field section of each of the modern Olympic games, a fact which has probably caused the erroneous belief just cited.

The tenth Olympiad will be held in Los Angeles, U.S.A., in 1932. Elaborate and comprehensive plans are being closely followed which are expected to make the second meet to be held in the New World one of the most successful ever to be staged. The games will start July 30th, and continue for sixteen days, ending August 14th.

CHAPTER IX

OLYMPIC GAMES ORGANIZATION

AT THE HEAD of the complicated system of organizations that control the destiny of the modern Olympic games stands the International Olympic committee. This body consists of sixty-eight members who represent forty-eight nations. The so-called major countries have three members each serving on this committee while the minor ones must worry along with one or two members, an arrangement that is far from being democratic.

The duties of the International Olympic committee are few and consist chiefly of naming the city where each Olympiad is to be held and delegating authority to a local committee for the actual work of preparing for and conducting the games. This body has set up the protocol, or constitution, under which the games are held every fourth year. It meets at call once a year, and so far, these meetings have always been held in Europe.

The object of the modern Olympic games as set forth in the words of the protocol is as follows: "The International Olympic committee, to whom the Congress of Paris entrusted the mission of watching over the development of the Olympic Games which were re-established on the 23rd of June, 1894, propose firstly to ensure the regular celebration of the Games; secondly, to make this celebration more and more perfect, worthy of its glorious past and conforming to the high ideals which inspire those who are urging on the revival of the Games; thirdly, to organize meetings and competitions and, in general to take all proper measures to conduct modern athletics in the right way."

Membership in the International Olympic committee is permanent, and the number of nations represented is unlimited. It is a self-perpetuating body.

The International committee still retains much the same organization as when it was first set up in 1895, with Baron Pierre de Courbetin as president. The Baron is now president *emeritus* while Count de Baillet-Latour of Brussels, Belgium, is the active president. The three representatives of the United States on this committee are the following: William May Garland of Los Angeles, General Charles H. Sherril of New York and Ernest Lee Jahnke of New Orleans. Mr. Garland is the ranking American member. The International Olympic committee maintains permanent headquarters at Lausanne, Switzerland.

Next in line to the International Olympic committee are the National Olympic committees. There is one National Olympic committee for each nation represented on the International Olympic committee. The chief duties of each National Olympic committee are to raise funds to meet the expenses of sending their athletes to the Olympiads, to designate locations for the final tryouts and to select national teams from these tryouts for participation in the Olympic games.

Supplementing the International Olympic committee and the National Olympic committees are a group of twenty international athletic organizations. Their actual connection with the various Olympic committees is somewhat vague. Each international organization is made up of the various national bodies governing each branch of amateur sport. For example, one organization governs international track and field athletics, another controls wrestling, another boxing, and so on. These international organizations establish the rules of competition, select officials and arrange the athletic program for each Olympiad. They also pass upon the eligibility of athletes for participation in the Olympic games.

The twenty international organizations are as follows: International Amateur federation, International Rowing federation, International Bobsleigh and Tobogganing federation, International Amateur Boxing federation, International Cyclists' union, International Horse-riding federation, International Fencing federation, International Association Football federation, International Gymnastic federation, International Amateur Handball federation, International Ice Hockey League, International Field Hockey federation, International Amateur Wrestling federation, Græco-Roman and Free, International Amateur Swimming federation, International Skating union, International Pelota federation, International Weight-lifting federation, International Ski federation, International Shooting union and International Yacht Racing union.

The ruling of these international organizations on Olympic eligibility is that each participating athlete must be a citizen of the country he represents and, having once competed for his native country, he can never compete under the flag of any other nation regardless of his subsequent citizenship or residence except in case of conquest or a new nation being created by treaty.

In addition to these duties, the international organizations certify to world and Olympic records. In short, they handle the multitude of details concerned with international amateur sport.

The definition of an amateur privileged to participate in the Olympic games is given in the Protocol of the International Olympic committee as follows: "Section 2. An athlete taking part in the Olympic games must satisfy the following conditions: Article 1; Must not be or knowingly have become, a professional in the sport for which he is entered or in any other sport. Article 2; Must not have received re-imbursement or compensation for loss of salary.

"Finally each athlete must sign the following declaration on his honor: 'I, the undersigned, declare on my honor that I am an amateur according to the Olympic Rules of Amateurism.'

"There is no age limit for competitors in the Olympic games."

The athletes winning the first three places in each event are awarded medals and diplomas; gold for the first place, silver for second place and bronze for third place. Three entries are allowed each nation in each individual event and one team is allowed each nation in team events.

Finally, we come to the Organizing committee, legally known as the "Xth Olympiade Committee of the Games of Los Angeles, U. S. A." The duties of this committee, which were delegated to it by the American Olympic association, consist of the actual financing of, preparation for and staging of the games of the Xth Olympiad. The personnel of this committee is: William May Garland, president; Harry J. Bauer, treasurer and Zack J. Farmer, general secretary and manager. The executive staff consists of the following: Gwynn Wilson, associate manager; William M. Henry, sports technical director; J. F. Mackenzie, ticket manager; H. O. Davis, director of Olympic village and William M. Creakbaum, manager of the press department.

This multiplicity of organizations may seem a bit confusing to the reader so let us work out a concrete example of how the system functions, say, in connection with the Xth Olympiad.

The International Olympic committee, having designated Los Angeles as the location of the Xth Olympiad, and being too loosely organized to actually conduct the games itself, invited the American Olympic committee to handle them. The American Olympic committee then started a financial campaign to raise funds to meet the expenses of the American athletes and designated Palo Alto, California, as the scene, on July 15-16, of the final American tryouts.

But inasmuch as the American Olympic committee itself is too loosely organized to prepare for and conduct the Xth Olympiad, it passed on to the Organizing committee the authority (which it had previously received from the International Olympic committee) to actually conduct the games.

In the background are the international athletic organizations which have no direct connection with the games save to pass upon the eligibility of the participating athletes and to determine the program of events.

So there is the Olympic games organization machine. It is somewhat complicated, to be sure, thereby giving rise to occasional misunderstandings, but, by and large, it functions smoothly and efficiently.

CHAPTER X

PROPOSED Xth OLYMPIAD PROGRAM

Los Angeles, California, U. S. A.
July 30 to August 14, 1932

LOCATION OF STADIA

Olympic Stadium — Located in Olympic Park in the heart of the Los Angeles metropolitan area, the Olympic Stadium, with a seating capacity of 105,000, will be the center of the various activities of the Xth Olympiad. Olympic Park is bounded on the north by Exposition boulevard, on the east by Figueroa street, on the south by Santa Barbara avenue and on the west by Vermont avenue.

Olympic Auditorium — 1801 South Grand avenue, Los Angeles.

Armory — Olympic Park, Los Angeles.

Rose Bowl — Pasadena, approximately eight miles north of Los Angeles.

Riviera — Country Club, located on Beverly boulevard approximately eighteen miles west of Los Angeles.

Yachting Course — Los Angeles Harbor (San Pedro), approximately twenty-two miles south of Los Angeles.

Swimming Stadium — Olympic Park, Los Angeles.

Marine Stadium — Long Beach, approximately twenty-five miles southeast of Los Angeles.

Rifle Range — Elysian Park, on North Broadway south of the Los Angeles river, Los Angeles.
(Note — "meter" is abbreviated to "m" in the following list of events.)

Date & Hour	EVENTS	PLACE
Saturday		
July 30, 1932		
2:30 p.m.	OPENING CEREMONY	Olympic Stadium
6:00 p.m.	WEIGHTLIFTING	Olympic Auditorium
Sunday		
July 31	ATHLETICS	Olympic Stadium
2:30 p.m.	400m low hurdles—Men (Trials)	
2:30 p.m.	High jump—Men	
2:30 p.m.	Shot put—Men	
3:00 p.m.	100m—Men (Trials)	
4:00 p.m.	800m—Men (Trials)	
4:30 p.m.	100m—Men (Trials)	
5:00 p.m.	400m low hurdles—Men (Trials)	
5:30 p.m.	Javelin—Women	
5:30 p.m.	10,000m—Men (Final)	
1:00 p.m.	WEIGHTLIFTING	Olympic Auditorium
7:00 p.m.	WEIGHTLIFTING	Olympic Auditorium
1:00 p.m.	FENCING (Foil Teams)	Armory
Monday		
August 1st	ATHLETICS	Olympic Stadium
2:30 p.m.	100m—Men (Semi-finals)	
2:30 p.m.	Hammer throw—Men	
3:00 p.m.	100m—Men (Finals)	
3:30 p.m.	400m low hurdles—Men (Final)	
3:45 p.m.	100m—Women (Trials)	
4:30 p.m.	800m—Men (Semi-finals)	
5:00 p.m.	100m—Women (Semi-finals)	
5:15 p.m.	3,000m steeple-chase—Men (Trials)	
9:00 a.m.	FENCING (Foil Teams)	Armory
1:00 p.m.	FENCING (Foil Teams)	Armory
11:00 a.m.	WRESTLING (Free Style)	Olympic Auditorium
6:00 p.m.	WRESTLING (Free Style)	Olympic Auditorium
7:30 p.m.	TRACK CYCLING	Rose Bowl
	1000m scratch (Trials)	
	2000m tandems (Trials)	
	1000m scratch (reclassification)	
	1000m by time (Trials)	
Tuesday		
August 2nd	ATHLETICS	Olympic Stadium
2:30 p.m.	110m high hurdles—Men (Trials)	
2:30 p.m.	Broad jump—Men	
2:30 p.m.	Discus—Women	
3:00 p.m.	200m—Men (Trials)	

Date & Hour	EVENTS	PLACE
3:45 p.m.	800m—Men (Final)	
4:00 p.m.	100m—Women (Final)	
4:15 p.m.	110m high hurdles—Men (Semi-finals)	
4:45 p.m.	5000m—Men (Trials)	
5:30 p.m.	200m—Men (Trials)	
1:00 p.m.	FENCING (Foil—Men and Women)	Armory
11:00 a.m.	WRESTLING (Free Style)	Olympic Auditorium
6:00 p.m.	WRESTLING (Free Style)	Olympic Auditorium
7:30 p.m.	TRACK CYCLING 1000m scratch (¼ finals) 1000m scratch (reclassification) 4000m pursuit race (Trials) 4000m pursuit race (¼ finals)	Rose Bowl
9:00 a.m.	PENTATHLON (Equestrian)	Riviera
Wednesday August 3rd	ATHLETICS	Olympic Stadium
2:30 p.m.	50,000m walk—Men (Start)	
2:30 p.m.	200m—Men (Semi-finals)	
2:30 p.m.	Pole vault—Men	
2:30 p.m.	Discus—Men	
3:00 p.m.	80m high hurdles—Women (Trials)	
3:45 p.m.	110m high hurdles—Men (Final)	
5:00 p.m.	200m—Men (Final)	
5:15 p.m.	1500m—Men (Trials)	
6:30 p.m.	50,000m walk—Men (Finish)	
11:00 a.m.	WRESTLING (Free Style)	Olympic Auditorium
6:00 p.m.	WRESTLING (Free Style) (Finals)	Olympic Auditorium
7:30 p.m.	TRACK CYCLING (Finals) 1000m scratch (semi-finals) 4000m pursuit race (semi-finals) 1000m scratch (Finals) 1000m scratch (for 3rd place) 4000m pursuit race (Finals) 4000m pursuit race (for 3rd place) 2000m tandems (Finals) 2000m tandems (for 3rd place)	Rose Bowl
8:00 a.m.	PENTATHLON (Fencing)	Armory
1:00 p.m.	PENTATHLON (Fencing)	Armory
Thursday August 4th	ATHLETICS	Olympic Stadium
2:30 p.m.	400m—Men (Trials)	
2:30 p.m.	Javelin—Men	

Date & Hour	Events	Place
2:30 p.m.	Hop, step and jump—Men	
3:30 p.m.	80m high hurdles—Women (Semi-finals)	
3:45 p.m.	1500m—Men (Final)	
4:00 p.m.	400m—Men (Trials)	
4:30 p.m.	80m high hurdles—Women (Final)	
1:00 p.m.	FENCING	Armory
11:00 a.m.	WRESTLING (Greco-Roman)	Olympic Auditorium
6:00 p.m.	WRESTLING (Greco-Roman)	Olympic Auditorium
8:00 a.m.	CYCLING—Road Race	
9:00 a.m.	PENTATHLON—Shooting	Rifle Range

Friday
August 5th

Date & Hour	Events	Place
10:00 a.m.	ATHLETICS	Olympic Stadium
	Decathlon—100m—Men	
11:00 a.m.	Decathlon—broad jump—Men	
	ATHLETICS	Olympic Stadium
2:30 p.m.	400m—Men (Semi-finals)	
2:30 p.m.	Decathlon—shot put—Men	
3:15 p.m.	5000m—Men (Final)	
3:30 p.m.	Decathlon—high jump—Men	
4:30 p.m.	400m—Men (Final)	
5:30 p.m.	Decathlon—400m—Men	
8:00 a.m.	FENCING (Sword Teams)	Armory
1:00 p.m.	FENCING (Sword Teams)	Armory
11:00 a.m.	WRESTLING (Greco-Roman)	Olympic Auditorium
6:00 p.m.	WRESTLING (Greco-Roman)	Olympic Auditorium
9:00 a.m.	PENTATHLON (Swimming)	Swimming Stadium
12:00 m.	YACHTING	L. A. Harbor

Saturday
August 6th

Date & Hour	Events	Place
10:00 a.m.	ATHLETICS	Olympic Stadium
	Decathlon—110m high hurdles—Men	
11:00 a.m.	Decathlon—discus—Men	
	ATHLETICS	Olympic Stadium
2:30 p.m.	4x100m relay—Men (Trials)	
2:30 p.m.	Decathlon—pole vault—Men	
3:15 p.m.	4x100m relay—Women (Trials)	
4:00 p.m.	3000m steeple chase—Men (Final)	
4:30 p.m.	Decathlon—Javelin—Men	
4:30 p.m.	4x400m relay—Men (Trials)	
5:30 p.m.	Decathlon—1500m—Men	
9:00 a.m.	FENCING (Sword Teams)	Armory
11:00 a.m.	WRESTLING (Greco-Roman)	Olympic Auditorium

Date & Hour	Events	Place
6:00 p.m.	WRESTLING (Greco-Roman)	Olympic Auditorium
9:00 a.m.	PENTATHLON—Cross Country run	
12:00 m.	YACHTING	L. A. Harbor
	SWIMMING	Swimming Stadium
9:00 a.m.	100m free style—Men (Trials)	
9:30 a.m.	200m breast stroke—Women (Trials)	
10:10 a.m.	Water Polo	
3:00 p.m.	100m free style—Women (Trials)	
3:30 p.m.	100m free style—Men (Semi-finals)	
3:40 p.m.	Water polo	
	FIELD HOCKEY	To be announced.

Sunday August 7th	ATHLETICS AND LACROSSE	Olympic Stadium
2:30 p.m.	High jump—Women	
2:30 p.m.	4x100m relay—Men (Semi-finals)	
3:00 p.m.	4x100m relay—Women (Final)	
3:30 p.m.	Marathon—Men (Start)	
3:30 p.m.	4x100m relay—Men (Final)	
3:45 p.m.	DEMONSTRATION OF LACROSSE	
4:30 p.m.	4x400m relay—Men (Final)	
6:05 p.m.	Marathon—Men (Finish)	
2:00 p.m.	FENCING (Sword Teams)	Armory
11:00 a.m.	WRESTLING (Greco-Roman)	Olympic Auditorium
6:00 p.m.	WRESTLING (Greco-Roman) (Finals)	Olympic Auditorium
12:00 m.	YACHTING	L. A. Harbor
	SWIMMING	Swimming Stadium
9:30 a.m.	200m Breast Stroke—Women	
9:50 a.m.	Water Polo	
3:00 p.m.	100m free style—Women (Semi-finals)	
3:30 p.m.	100m free style—Men (Final)	
3:45 p.m.	Water Polo	

Monday August 8th		
8:00 a.m.	GYMNASTICS	Olympic Stadium
2:30 p.m.	FIELD HOCKEY (Semi-finals)	Olympic Stadium
8:00 p.m.	DEMONSTRATION (American Football)	Olympic Stadium
9:00 a.m.	FENCING (Swords)	Armory
1:00 p.m.	FENCING (Swords)	Armory
12:00 m.	YACHTING	L. A. Harbor

Date & Hour	EVENTS	PLACE
	SWIMMING	Swimming Stadium
8:30 a.m.	Spring board diving—Men (Final)	
11:30 a.m.	Relay 4x200m—Men (Trials)	
12:00 m.	Water Polo	
3:00 p.m.	100m free style—Women (Final)	
3:15 p.m.	400m free style—Men (Trials)	
4:10 p.m.	Water Polo	

Tuesday
August 9th

8:00 a.m.	GYMNASTICS	Olympic Stadium
2:30 p.m.	LACROSSE	Olympic Stadium
1:00 p.m.	FENCING (Swords)	Armory
12:00 m.	YACHTING	L. A. Harbor
	SWIMMING	Swimming Stadium
10:00 a.m.	400m free style—Men (Semi-finals)	
10:30 a.m.	100m breast stroke—Women (Trials)	
11:00 a.m.	Water Polo	
3:00 p.m.	Exhibition of spring board diving— Men (3 first placed)	
3:30 p.m.	Relay 4x200m—Men (Final)	
4:00 p.m.	200m breast stroke—Women (Final)	
4:20 p.m.	Water Polo	
8:00 a.m.	ROWING	Long Beach
1:00 p.m.	ROWING	Long Beach
2:00 p.m.	BOXING	Olympic Auditorium
8:00 p.m.	BOXING	Olympic Auditorium

Wednesday
August 10th

8:00 a.m.	GYMNASTICS	Olympic Stadium
3:00 p.m.	GYMNASTICS	Olympic Stadium
8:00 p.m.	GYMNASTICS (Demonstration)	Olympic Stadium
8:00 a.m.	FENCING (Sabre)	Armory
1:00 p.m.	FENCING (Sabre)	Armory
12:00 m.	YACHTING	L. A. Harbor
	SWIMMING	Swimming Stadium
8:30 a.m.	Springboard diving—Women (Final)	
11:30 a.m.	100m back stroke—Men (Trials)	
12:00 m.	Relay 4x100m—Women (Trials)	
12:20 p.m.	Water Polo	
3:00 p.m.	Spring board diving exhibition— Women (3 first placed)	
3:30 p.m.	400m free style—Men (Final)	

Date & Hour	Events	Place
3:50 p.m.	100m back stroke—Women (Semi-finals)	
4:10 p.m.	Water Polo	
8:00 a.m.	ROWING	Long Beach
1:00 p.m.	ROWING	Long Beach
9:00 a.m.	BOXING	Olympic Auditorium
2:00 p.m.	BOXING	Olympic Auditorium
8:00 p.m.	BOXING	Olympic Auditorium
8:00 a.m.	EQUESTRIAN SPORTS (Dressage)	Riviera
2:00 p.m.	EQUESTRIAN SPORTS (Dressage)	Riviera

Thursday
August 11th

8:00 a.m.	GYMNASTICS	Olympic Stadium
2:30 p.m.	FIELD HOCKEY (Finals)	Olympic Stadium
1:00 p.m.	FENCING (Sabre)	Armory
12:00 m.	YACHTING	L. A. Harbor
	SWIMMING	Swimming Stadium
10:00 a.m.	400m free style—Women (Trials)	
10:30 a.m.	1500m free style—Men (Trials 1 and 2)	
11:30 a.m.	Water Polo	
3:00 p.m.	1500m free style—Men (Trials 3)	
3:30 p.m.	200m back stroke—Men (Trials)	
4:00 p.m.	100m back stroke—Men (Semi-finals)	
4:15 p.m.	100m back stroke—Women (Final)	
4:30 p.m.	Water Polo	
8:00 a.m.	ROWING	Long Beach
1:00 p.m.	ROWING	Long Beach
9:00 a.m.	BOXING	Olympic Auditorium
2:00 p.m.	BOXING	Olympic Auditorium
8:00 p.m.	BOXING	Olympic Auditorium
8:00 a.m.	EQUESTRIAN SPORTS (Dressage)	Riviera
2:00 p.m.	EQUESTRIAN SPORTS (Dressage)	Riviera

Friday
August 12th

8:00 a.m.	GYMNASTICS	Olympic Stadium
2:30 p.m.	LACROSSE	Olympic Stadium
8:00 a.m.	FENCING	Armory
1:00 p.m.	FENCING	Armory

Date & Hour	EVENTS	PLACE
12:00 m.	YACHTING	L. A. Harbor
	SWIMMING	Swimming Stadium
9:00 a.m.	High diving—Women (Final)	
11:30 a.m.	400m free style—Women (semi-finals)	
11:55 a.m.	Water Polo	
3:00 p.m.	200m breast stroke—Men (Semi-finals)	
3:20 p.m.	1500m free style—Men (Semi-finals)	
4:20 p.m.	100m back stroke—Men (Final)	
4:35 p.m.	Relay race 4x100m—Women (Final)	
4:55 p.m.	Water Polo	
8:00 a.m.	ROWING	Long Beach
1:00 p.m.	ROWING	Long Beach
2:00 p.m.	BOXING	Olympic Auditorium
8:00 p.m.	BOXING	Olympic Auditorium
8:00 a.m.	EQUESTRIAN SPORTS—Steeple	To be announced.
9:00 a.m.	SHOOTING—Pistol	Rifle Range
2:00 p.m.	SHOOTING—Pistol	Rifle Range
Saturday August 13th		
2:00 p.m.	EQUESTRIAN—Jumps	Olympic Stadium
1:00 p.m.	FENCING (Sabre)	Armory
	SWIMMING	Swimming Stadium
9:00 a.m.	High diving—Men (Final)	
12:00 m.	Water Polo	
3:00 p.m.	Exhibition of high diving—Men (3 first placed)	
3:30 p.m.	200m breast stroke—Men (Final)	
3:45 p.m.	400m free style—Women (Final)	
4:00 p.m.	1500m free style—Men (Final)	
4:30 p.m.	Exhibition of high diving—Women (3 first placed)	
5:00 p.m.	Water Polo	
2:00 p.m.	BOXING	Olympic Auditorium
8:00 p.m.	BOXING	Olympic Auditorium
1:00 p.m.	ROWING	Long Beach
9:00 a.m.	SHOOTING—Min. carbine	Rifle Range
2:00 p.m.	SHOOTING—Min. carbine	Rifle Range
Sunday August 14th		
1:00 p.m.	EQUESTRIAN SPORTS—Jumps	Olympic Stadium
5:00 p.m.	CLOSING CEREMONY	Olympic Stadium

Chapter XI

OLYMPIC AND WORLD RECORDS

Locale of Modern Olympiads and Winners

(Note — It should be borne in mind that the controlling International Olympiad Committee recognizes only individual championships, hence no nation can become the official champion of any Olympiad. Through various systems of awarding points, however, one nation is accorded the unofficial championship. Because the United States and European nations are usually at odds over the method of awarding points, there is no definite rule for determining the national winner. Often two or more countries will claim the championship. The following table gives the generally accepted unofficial national championships of the first nine Olympiads.)

Olympiad	Year	Where Held	Winner
Ist Olympiad	1896	Athens, Greece	U. S. A.
IInd Olympiad	1900	Paris, France	U. S. A.
IIIrd Olympiad	1904	St. Louis, U. S. A.	U. S. A.
IVth Olympiad	1906	Athens, Greece	U. S. A.
Vth Olympiad	1908	London, Gr. Brit.	Gr. Brit.
VIth Olympiad	1912	Stockholm, Sweden	Sweden
VIIth Olympiad	1920	Antwerp, Belgium	U. S. A.

(The VIIth Olympiad was scheduled originally for Berlin, Germany, in 1916, but was not held because of the World War.)

VIIIth Olympiad	1924	Paris, France	U. S. A.
IXth Olympiad	1928	Amsterdam, Hol.	Germany
Xth Olympiad	1932	Los Angeles, U. S. A.	(? ? ?)

Modern Pentathlon

The modern Pentathlon consists of the following:

Target shooting — pistol and rifle, distance 25 meters or 27.34 yards.

Swimming, free style — distance 300 meters or 328.09 yds.

Fencing — duelling.

Riding, horseback — 5000 meters or 5465 yds. or 3.105 m.

Cross country run — 4000 meters or 4372 yds. or 2.484 m.

The Decathlon

The decathlon (from the Greek *deca*, a combining form meaning ten, and *thlon*, meaning contest) is a contest that would have delighted the hearts of the ancient Greeks. They believed in harmonious athletic development and certainly no one can hope to win this "one-man-track-team" event unless he is an all-round athlete.

It was introduced into the modern Olympic games in 1912. The ten events are as follows: 100-meter sprint, 400-meter race, 1500-meter race, 110-meter high hurdle race, running high jump, running broad jump, pole vault, shot put, discus throw, and javelin throw.

Comparative Tables

1 meter = 39.3696 inches, or 3.2808 feet, or 1.0936 yards.

100 meters = 109.36 yards.

110 meters = 120.23 yards.

200 meters = 218.6 yards.

400 meters = 437.2 yards or 2.8 yards less than a quarter mile.

800 meters = 874.4 yards or 5.6 yards less than a half mile.

1500 meters = 1639.5 yards or 120.5 yards less than a mile.

1600 meters = 1748.8 yards or 11.2 yards less than a mile.

3000 meters = 3279 yards or 1.863 miles.

5000 meters = 5465 yards or 3.105 miles.

10000 meters = 10,930 yards or 6.210 miles.

1 yard = 3 feet or 36 inches or 0.9144 meters.

1 mile = 5280 feet, or 1760 yards or 1609.3 meters.

Art Section

The art section of the Olympics consists of painting, music, literature, sculpture and architecture.

OLYMPIC RECORDS

Event	Time or Distance	Winner and Nation	Where Made	Date
100 meters	10.6s	D. F. Lippincott, U.S.A.	Stockholm	1912
	(Trial Heat)	H. M. Abrahams, Gt. Br.	Paris	1924
	(Trial Heat)	Percy Williams, Canada	Amsterdam	1928
	(Trial Heat)	R. F. McAllister, U.S.A.	Amsterdam	1928
		J. E. London, Gt. Br.	Amsterdam	1928
200 meters	21.6s	A. Hahn, U.S.A.	St. Louis	1904
	(Trial Heat)	J. V. Scholz, U.S.A.	Paris	1924
		Helmut Kornig, Germany	Amsterdam	1928
400 meters	47.6s	E. H. Liddell, Gt. Br.	Paris	1924
800 meters	1m. 51 4-5s.	D. G. A. Lowe, Gt. Br.	Amsterdam	1928
1,500 meters	3m. 53 1-5s.	H. E. Larva, Finland	Amsterdam	1928
5,000 meters	14m. 31.2s.	Paavo Nurmi, Finland	Paris	1924
10,000 meters	30m. 18 4-5s.	Paavo Nurmi, Finland	Amsterdam	1928
10,000 meters (Walk)	46m. 28.4s.	G. H. Goulding, Canada	Stockholm	1912
110 meter Hurdles	14 3-5s (Trial Heat).	Weightman-Smith, S. Africa	Amsterdam	1928
400 meter Hurdles	53 2-5s.	Lord Burghley, Gr. Bt.	Amsterdam	1928
400 meter Hurdles	53 2-5s (Trial Heat).	F. M. Taylor, U.S.A.	Amsterdam	1928
High Jump	6ft. 6in.	H. M. Osborn, U.S.A.	Paris	1924
Broad Jump	25ft. 4 3-4in.	E. B. Hamm, U.S.A.	Amsterdam	1928
Hop, Step, Jump	50ft. 11 1-4in.	A. W. Winter, Australia	Paris	1924
Pole Vault	13ft. 9 3-8in.	Sabin W. Carr, U.S.A.	Amsterdam	1928
Discus	155ft. 2 15-16in.	Dr. C. L. Houser, U.S.A.	Amsterdam	1928
Javelin	218ft. 6 1-4 in.	E. H. Lundquist, Sweden.	Amsterdam	1928
16-lb. Shot	52ft. 11-16in.	John Kuck, U.S.A.	Amsterdam	1928
16-lb. Hammer	179ft. 8 4in	M. J. McGrath, U.S.A.	Stockholm	1912
56-lb. Weight	36ft. 11 1-2in.	P. J. McDonald, U.S.A.	Antwerp	1920
Pentathlon	14 points.	E. R. Lehtonen, Finland	Antwerp	1920
Decathlon	8056.20 points.	Paavo Yrjola, Finland	Amsterdam	1928

400 meter Relay   41s.   United States team — Frank Hussey, L. A. Clark, Loren Murchison, J. A. Leconey, Paris, 1924. United States team — Frank Wykoff, James F. Quinn, Charles E. Borah, Henry A. Russell, Amsterdam, 1928.

1600 meter Relay   3m. 14 1-5s.   United States team — George Baird, Fred Alderman, Emerson Spencer, Raymond J. Barbuti, Amsterdam, 1928.

3000 meter team race   8m. 32s.   Finland team — Paavo Nurmi, Willie Ritola, E. Katz, Paris, 1924.

OLYMPIC SWIMMING RECORDS (MEN)

DISTANCE	TIME	HOLDER AND NATION	WHERE MADE	DATE
100 meters, f. style	58 3-5s.	John Weissmuller, U.S.A.	Amsterdam	1928
400 meters, f. style	5m. 1 3-5s.	Albert Zorilla, Argentine	Amsterdam	1928
1,500 meters, f. style	19m. 51 2-5s.	Arne Borg, Sweden	Amsterdam	1928
100 meters, ba. stroke	1m. 8.1s.	George Kojac, U.S.A.	Amsterdam	1928
200 meters, br. stroke	2m. 48 4-5s.	Y. Tsuruta, Japan	Amsterdam	1928
400 meters, br. stroke	6m. 29 3-5s.	W. Bathe, Germany	Stockholm	1912
800 meters Relay	9m. 36 1-5s.	United States team	Amsterdam	1928

(Austin Clapp, Walter Laufer, George Kojac, John Weissmuller)

OLYMPIC SWIMMING RECORDS (WOMEN)

DISTANCE	TIME	HOLDER AND NATION	WHERE MADE	DATE
100 meters, f. style	1m. 11s.	Albina Osipowich, U.S.A.	Amsterdam	1928
300 meters, f. style	4m. 34s.	Ethelda Bleibtrey, U.S.A.	Antwerp	1920
400 meters, f. style	5m. 42 2-5s.	Martha Norelius, U.S.A.	Amsterdam	1928
100 meters, ba. stroke	1m. 22s.	Marie Braun, Holland	Amsterdam	1928
200 meters, br. stroke	3m. 11 1-5s.	Hilda Schrader, Germany	Amsterdam	1928
400 meter Relay	4m. 47 3-5s.	United States team	Amsterdam	1928

(Adelaide Lambert, Eleanor Garatti, Martha Norelius, Albina Osipowich)

EVENT WINNERS OF MODERN OLYMPICS

1896—ATHENS	1906—ATHENS	1920—ANTWERP
1900—PARIS	1908—LONDON	1924—PARIS
1904—ST. LOUIS	1912—STOCKHOLM	1928—AMSTERDAM

TRACK AND FIELD

60-METER RUN

1900	A. E. Kraenzlein, U.S.A.	7s
1904	Archie Hahn, U.S.A.	7s

100-METER RUN

1896	T. E. Burke, U.S.A.	12s
1900	F. W. Jarvis, U.S.A.	10 4-5s
1904	Archie Hahn, U.S.A.	11s
1906	Archie Hahn, U.S.A.	11 1-5s
1908	R. E. Walker, S. Af.	10 4-5s
1912	R. C. Craig, U.S.A.	10 4-5s
1920	C. W. Paddock, U.S.A.	10 4-5s
1924	H. M. Abrahams, Gt. Br.	10.6s
1928	Percy Williams, Canada	10 4-5s

200-METER RUN

1900	J. W. B. Tewksbury, U.S.A.	22 1-5s
1904	Archie Hahn, U.S.A.	21 3-5s
1908	R. Kerr, Canada	22 2-5s
1912	R. C. Craig, U.S.A.	21.7s
1920	Allan Woodring, U.S.A.	22s
1924	J. V. Scholz, U.S.A.	21.6s
1928	Percy Williams, Canada	21 4-5s

400-METER RUN

1896	T. E. Burke, U.S.A.	54 1-5s
1900	M. W. Long, U.S.A.	49 2-5s
1904	H. L. Hillman, U.S.A.	49 1-5s
1906	Paul Pilgrim, U.S.A.	53 1-5s
1908	W. Halswelle, Gt. Br.	50s
1912	C. D. Reidpath, U.S.A.	48.2s
1920	B. G. D. Rudd, S. Af.	49 3-5s
1924	E. H. Liddell, Gr. Br.	47 6s
1928	R. J. Barbuti, U.S.A.	47 4-5s

800-METER RUN

1896	E. H. Flack, Gt. Br.	2m. 11s
1900	A. E. Tysoe, Gt. Br.	2m. 1 2-5s
1904	J. D. Lightbody, U.S.A.	1m. 56s
1906	Paul Pilgrim, U.S.A.	2m. 1 1-5s
1908	M. W. Sheppard, U.S.A.	1m. 52 4-5s
1912	J. E. Meredith, U.S.A.	1m. 51.9s
1920	A. G. Hill, Gt. Br.	1m. 53 2-5s
1924	D. G. A. Lowe, Gt. Br.	1m. 52.4s
1928	D. G. A. Lowe, Gt. Br.	1m. 51 4-5s

1,500-METER RUN

1896	E. H. Flack, Gt. Br.	4m. 33 1-5s
1900	C. Bennett, Gt. Br.	4m. 6s
1904	J. D. Lightbody, U.S.A.	4m. 5 2-5s
1906	J. D. Lightbody, U.S.A.	4m. 12s
1908	M. W. Sheppard, U.S.A.	4m. 3 2-5s
1912	A. N. S. Jackson Gt. Br.	3m. 56.8s
1920	A. G. Hill, Gt. Br.	4m. 1 4-5s
1924	Paavo Nurmi, Finland	3m. 53.6s
1928	H. E. Larva, Finland	3m. 53 1-5s

5,000-METER RUN

1912	H. Kolehmainen, Finland	14m. 36.6s
1920	J. Guillemot, France	14m. 55 3-5s
1924	Paavo Nurmi, Finland	14m. 31.2s
1928	Willie Ritola, Finland	14m. 38s

5-MILE RUN

1906	H. Hawtrey, Gt. Br.	26m 26 1-5s
1908	E. R. Voigt, Gt. Br.	25m. 11 1-5s

10,000-METER RUN

1912	H. Kolehmainen, Finland	31m. 20.8s
1920	Paavo Nurmi, Finland	31m. 45 4-5s
1924	Willie Ritola, Finland	30m. 23.2s
1928	Paavo Nurmi, Finland	30m. 18 4-5s

MARATHON
(26 miles 385 yards — 42.263 Kilometers)

1896	S. Loues, Greece	2h. 55m. 20s
1900	Teato, France	2h. 59m
1904	T. J. Hicks, U.S.A.	3h. 28m. 53s
1906	W. J. Sherring, Can.	2h. 51m. 23 3-5s
1908	John J. Hayes, U.S.A.	2h. 55m. 18s
1912	K. K. McArthur, S. Af.	2h. 36m. 54.8s
1920	Kolehmainen, Finland	2h. 32m. 35 4-5s
1924	A. O Stenroos, Finland	2h. 41m. 22.6s
1928	El Oaufi, France	2h. 32m. 57s

110-METER HURDLES

1896	Curtis, U.S.A.	17 3-5s
1900	A. C. Kraenzlein, U.S.A.	15 2-5s
1904	F. W. Schule, U.S.A.	16s
1906	R. G. Leavitt, U.S.A.	16 1-5s
1908	Forrest Smithson, U.S.A.	15s
1912	F. W. Kelly, U.S.A.	15.1s
1920	E. J. Thomson, Canada	14 4-5s
1924	D. C. Kinsey, U.S.A.	15s
1928	S. J. M. Atkinson, S. Af.	14 4-5s

200-METER HURDLES

1900	A. C. Kraenzlein, U.S.A.	25 2-5s
1904	H. L. Hillman U.S.A.	24 3-5s

400-METER HURDLES

1900	J. W. Tewksbury, U.S.A.	57 3-5s
1904	H. L. Hillman, U.S.A.	53s
1908	C. J. Bacon, U.S.A.	55s
1920	F. F Loomis, U.S.A.	54s
1924	F. M. Taylor, U.S.A.	*52.6s
1928	Lord Burghley, Gt. Br.	53 2-5s

*Not a record; one hurdle down.

2,500-METER STEEPLECHASE

1900	G. W. Orton, U.S.A.	7m. 34s
1904	J. D. Lightbody, U.S.A.	7m. 39 3-5s

3,000-METER STEEPLECHASE

1920	P. Hodge, Gt. Br.	10m. 2 2-5s
1924	Willie Ritola, Finland	9m. 33.6s
1928	T. A. Loukola, Finland	9m. 21 4-5s

3,200-METER STEEPLECHASE

1908	A. Russell, Gt. Br.	10m. 47 4-5s

4,000-METER STEEPLECHASE

1900	C. Rimmer, Gt. Br.	12m. 58 2-5s

CROSS-COUNTRY RUN

1912	H. Kolehmainen, Finland	45m. 11.6s

10,000-METER CROSS-COUNTRY RUN

1920	Paavo Nurmi, Finland	27m. 15s
1924	Paavo Nurmi, Finland	32m. 54.8s

1,500-METER WALK

1906	George V. Bonhag, U S.A.	7m. 12 3-5s

3,000-METER WALK

1920	Ugo Frigerio, Italy	13m. 14 1-5s

3,500-METER WALK

1908	G. E. Larner, Gt. Br.	14m. 55s

10,000-METER WALK

1912	G. H. Goulding, Canada	46m. 28 4s
1920	Ugo Frigerio, Italy	48m. 6 1-5s
1924	Ugo Frigerio, Italy	47m. 49s

10-MILE WALK

1908	G. E. Larner, Gt. Br.	1h. 15m. 57 2-5s

400-METER RELAY (4x100)

1912	Great Britain	42.4s
1920	U. S. A.	42 1-5s
1924	U. S. A.	41s
1928	U. S. A.	41s

1,600-METER RELAY (4x400)

1908	U. S. A.	3m. 27 1-5s
1912	U. S. A.	3m. 16.6s
1920	Great Britain	3m. 22 1-5s
1924	U. S. A.	3m. 16s
1928	U S. A.	3m. 14 1-5s

POLE VAULT

1896	W. W. Hoyt, U.S.A.	10ft. 9 3-4in
1900	I. K. Baxter, U.S.A.	10ft. 9 9-10in
1904	C. E. Dvorak, U.S.A.	11ft. 6in
1906	Gouder, France	11ft. 6in
1908	{ A. C. Gilbert, U.S.A. } { E. T. Cook Jr., U.S.A. }	12ft. 2in
1912	H. J. Babcock, U.S.A.	3.95m
1920	F. K. Foss, U.S.A.	4.09m
1924	{ L. S. Barnes, U.S.A. } { Glenn Graham, U.S.A. }	3.95m
1928	S. W. Carr, U.S.A.	4.20m

RUNNING HIGH JUMP

1896	E. H. Clark, U.S.A.	5ft. 11 1-4in
1900	I. K. Baxter, U.S.A.	6ft. 2 4-5in
1904	S. S. Jones, U.S.A.	5ft. 11in
1906	Con Leahy, Ireland	5ft. 9 7-8in
1908	H F. Porter, U.S.A.	6ft. 3in
1912	A. W. Richards, U.S.A.	1.93m
1920	R. W. Landon, U.S.A.	1.94m
1924	H. M. Osborn, U.S.A.	1.98m
1928	R. W. King, U.S.A.	1.94m

STANDING HIGH JUMP

1900	R. C. Ewry, U.S.A.	5ft. 5in
1904	R. C. Ewry, U S.A.	4ft. 11in
1906	R. C. Ewry, U.S.A.	5ft. 1 5-8in
1908	R. C. Ewry, U.S.A.	1.63m

RUNNING BROAD JUMP

1896	E. H. Clark, U.S.A.	20ft. 9 3-4in
1900	Kraenzlein, U.S.A.	23ft. 6 7-8in
1904	Myer Prinstein, U.S.A.	24ft. 1in
1906	Prinstein, U S A.	23ft. 7 1-2in
1908	Frank Irons, U.S.A.	24ft. 6 1-2in
1912	A. L. Gutterson, U.S.A.	7.60m
1920	Wm. Pettersen, Sweden	7.15m
1924	DeHart Hubbard, U.S.A.	7.445m
1928	E. B. Hamm, U.S.A.	7.73m

STANDING BROAD JUMP

1900	R. C. Ewry, U.S.A.	10ft. 6 2-5in
1904	R. C. Ewry, U.S.A.	11ft. 4 7-8in
1906	R. C. Ewry, U S.A.	10ft. 10in
1908	R. C. Ewry, U.S A.	10ft. 11 1-4in
1912	C. Tsicilitiras, Greece	3.37m

RUNNING HOP, STEP AND JUMP

1896	J. B. Connolly, U.S.A.	45ft
1900	Prinstein, U.S A.	47ft. 4 1-4in
1904	Myer Prinstein, U.S.A.	47ft
1906	P. O'Connor, Ireland	46ft. 2in
1908	T. J. Ahearne, Gt. Br.	48ft. 11 1-4in
1912	G. Lindblom, Sweden	14.76m
1920	V. Tuulos, Finland	14.505m
1924	A. W. Winter, Australia	15.525m
1928	Mikio Oda, Japan	15.21m

STANDING HOP, STEP AND JUMP

1900	R. C Ewry, U.S.A.	34ft. 8 1-2in
1904	R. C. Ewry, U.S.A.	34ft. 7 1-4in

16-LB. HAMMER THROW

1900	J. J. Flanagan, U.S.A.	167ft. 4in
1904	J. J. Flanagan, U.S.A.	168ft. 1in
1908	J. J. Flanagan, U.S A.	170ft. 4 1-4in
1912	M. J. McGrath, U.S.A.	54.74m.
1920	P. J. Ryan, U S.A.	52.875in
1924	F. D. Tootell, U.S.A.	53.295m
1928	Dr. Pat. O'Callaghan, Ireland	51.39m

56-POUND WEIGHT THROW

1904	E. Desmarteau, Canada	34ft. 4in
1920	P. J. McDonald, U.S.A.	11.265m

16-Lb. Shot Put

1896	R. S. Garrett, U.S.A.........36ft. 2in
1900	R Sheldon, U.S.A.........46ft. 3 1-8in
1904	Ralph Rose, U S.A.........48ft. 7in
1906	M J. Sheridan, U.S.A.....40ft. 4 4-5in
1908	Ralph Rose, U.S.A. 46ft. 7 1-2in
1912	P. J. McDonald, U.S.A.. ... 15.34m
	Right and left hand — Ralph
	Rose, U S.A... .. ..27.57m
1920	V. Porhola, Finland.........14.81m
1924	Clarence Houser, U.S.A........14.995m
1928	John Kuck, U S.A..........15.87m

Discus Throw

1896	R S. Garrett, U.S.A.. ....95ft. 7 1-2in
1900	Bauer, Hungary......118ft. 2 9-10in
1904	Sheridan, U.S A. 128ft. 10 1-2in
1906	M. J. Sheridan, U S A......136ft. 1-3in
1908	M. J. Sheridan, U.S.A........134ft. 2in
1912	A. R. Taipale, Finland 45.21m
	Right and left hand—A. R.
	Taipale, Finland 82.86m
1920	E. Niklander, Finland........44.685m
1924	Dr. C. L. Houser, U.S.A.......46.155m
1928	Dr. C. L. Houser, U.S.A........47.32m

Discus, Grecian Style

1906	W. Jaervinen, Finland.......115ft. 4in
1908	M. J. Sheridan, U.S.A....... 124ft. 8in

Javelin Throw

1906	E. Lemming, Sweden........175ft. 6in
1908	E. Lemming, Sweden.....178ft. 7 1-2in
	Held in middle—E. Lemming
	Sweden.................179ft. 10 1-2in
1912	E. Lemming. Sweden 60.64m
	Right and left hand—J. J.
	Saaristo, Finland 109.42m
1920	Jonni Myyra, Finland.........65.78m
1924	Jonni Myyra, Finland 62.96m
1928	E. H. Lundquist, Sweden.......66.60m

Pentathlon

1906	H. Mellander, Sweden.........24 pts
1912	F. R. Bie, Norway. ....16 pts
1920	E. R. Lehtonen, Finland........14 pts
1924	E. R. Lehtonen, Finland........16 pts

Decathlon

1912	Wieslander, Sweden......7,724.495 pts
1920	H. Lovland Norway......6,804.35 pts
1924	H. M. Osborn, U S A ....7,710.775 pts
1928	Paavo Yrjola, Finland.....8,056.20 pts

Modern Pentathlon

1912	C. Lilliehock, Sweden
1920	J. Dyrssen, Sweden
1924	O. Ludmann, Sweden
1928	S. A. Thofelt, Sweden

WRESTLING

(Catch-As-Catch-Can)

Flyweight

1904	R. Curry, U.S.A. (105-lb. class)

Bantamweight

1904	George Mehnert, U.S.A. (115-lb. class)
1908	G. N. Mehnert, U.S.A. (119-lb. class)
1924	Kustaa Pihalajamaki, Finland.
1928	K. Makinen, Finland.

Featherweight

1904	I. Niflot, U.S.A.
1908	G. S. Dole, U.S.A.
1920	Charles E. Ackerly, U.S.A.
1924	Robin Reed, U.S.A.
1928	Allie Morrison, U.S.A.

Lightweight

1904	B. J. Bradshaw, U.S.A.
1908	G. de Relwyskow, Great Britain.
1920	Kalle Antilla, Finland.
1924	Russell Vis, U S.A.
1928	O. Kapp, Esthonia.

Welterweight

1904	O. F. Roehm, U.S.A.
1924	Herman Gehri, Switzerland.
1928	A. J. Haavisto, Finland.

Middleweight

1904	Charles Erickson, U.S.A.
1908	S. V. Bacon, Great Britain.
1920	L. Leino, Finland.
1924	Fritz Haggmann, Switzerland.
1928	E. Kyburg, Switzerland.

Light Heavyweight

1924	John Spellman, U.S.A.
1928	T. S. Sjostedt, Sweden.

Heavyweight

1904	B. Hansen, U S.A.
1908	G. C. O'Kelly, Great Britain.
1920	R. Rotte, Switzerland.
1924	Harry Steele, U.S.A.
1928	J. C. Richthoff, Sweden.

WRESTLING

(Greco-Roman)

Bantamweight

1924	Edward Putsep, Esthonia.
1928	K. Leucht, Germany.

Featherweight

1912	Kalle Koskelo, Finland.
1920	Eriman. Finland.
1924	Kalle Antilla, Finland.
1928	V. Wali, Esthonia.

Lightweight

1906	Watzl, Austria.
1908	E. Porro, Italy.
1912	E. E. Ware, Finland.
1920	Vare, Finland.
1924	Oskari Friman, Finland.
1928	L. Keresztes, Hungary.

WELTERWEIGHT

1920 J. Johannsson, Sweden.

MIDDLEWEIGHT

1906 W. Weckman, Finland.
1908 F. M. Martenson, Sweden (161-lb. class)
1912 C. E. Johansson, Sweden.
1920 W. Westergren, Sweden.
1924 Edward Westerlund, Finland.
1928 V. A. Kokkinen, Finland.

LIGHT HEAVYWEIGHT

1908 W. Weckman, Finland
1912 A. O. Ahlgren, Sweden.
1924 C. O. Westergren, Sweden.
1928 S. Moustafa, Egypt.

HEAVYWEIGHT

1906 J. Jensen, Denmark.
1908 R. Wersz, Hungary.
1912 U. Soarela, Finland.
1920 Lindfors, Sweden.
1924 Henri DeGlane, France.
1928 J. R. Svensson, Sweden.

BOXING

FLYWEIGHT

1904 George V. Finnegan, U.S.A. (105-lb. class).
1920 Frank De Genero, U.S.A.
1924 Fidel La Barba, U.S.A.
1928 Anton Kocsis, Hungary.

BANTAMWEIGHT

1904 O. L. Kirk, U.S.A. (115-lb. class).
1920 Walter. South America.
1924 W. H. Smith, South Africa.
1928 Vittorio Tamagnini, Italy.

FEATHERWEIGHT

1904 O. L. Kirk, U.S.A.
1920 Fritsch, France.
1924 John Fields, U.S.A.
1928 L. Van Klaveren, Holland.

LIGHTWEIGHT

1904 H. J. Spanger, U.S.A.
1920 Samuel Mosberg, U.S.A.
1924 Harold Nielsen, Denmark.
1928 Carlo Orlandi, Italy.

WELTERWEIGHT

1904 Al Young, U.S.A.
1920 Schneider, Canada.
1924 J. S. Delarge, Belgium.
1928 Edward Morgan, New Zealand.

MIDDLEWEIGHT

1904 Charles Mayer, U.S.A.
1920 H. W. Mallin, Great Britain.
1924 H. W. Mallin, Great Britain.
1928 Piero Toscani, Italy.

LIGHT HEAVYWEIGHT

1920 Edward Eagan, U.S.A.
1924 H. J. Mitchell, Great Britain.
1928 Victoria Avendano, Argentina.

HEAVYWEIGHT

1904 Sam Berger, U.S.A.
1920 Rawson, Great Britain.
1924 O. Von Porat, Norway.
1928 Jurido Rodriguez, Argentina.

CYCLING

1906

333-1/3 Meters Race, Verri, Italy.
1000 Meters Race, Verri, Italy.
Tandem Race, 2000 Meters, Matthews and Rushen, Great Britain.
5000 Meters Race, Verri, Italy.
  20 Kilometer Paced Race, Pett.
  84 Kilometer Road Race, Vast and Bardonneau, France.

1908

One Lap (660 Yards), V. L. Johnson, Gt. Br.
5000 Meters, Ben Jones, Great Britain.
  20 Kilometers, C. B. Kingsbury, Gt. Br.
  100 Kilometers, C. H. Bartlett, Great Britain.
Three Laps Pursuit, L. Meredith, B Jones, E. Payne and C. B. Kingsbury, Gt. Br.
2000 Meters Tandem, M. Schilles and A. Auffray, France.

1912

Road Race, Individual, Rudolph Lewis, South Africa.
Team, Sweden.

1920

1000 Meters Race, Peeter, Holland.
2000 Meters Tandem Race, Ryan and Lance, Great Britain.
4000 Meters Race, Italy.
  50 Kilometers Race, Henry George, Belgium.
  160 Kilometers Team Race, Stenquist, Sweden.

1924

1000 Meters Race, Lucien Michaud, France.
2000 Meters Race Tandem, Cugnot and Lucien Choury, France.
4000 Meters Team Pursuit, Alfredo Dinale, Francesci Zucchetti, Angelo De Martini, Alerado Menegazzi, Italy.
  50 Kilometers Race, Jacobus Willem, Holland.
  188 Kilometers Road, Team, France.
  188 Kilometers Road, Individual, Armand Blanchonnet, France.

1928

1000 Meters Scratch, Beaufrand, France.
  2 Kilometers Tandem Lenne, Van Dyk, Holland.
Team-Pursuit Race, Italy.
Road Race, H. Hansen, Denmark.

GYMNASTICS

1904

Club Swinging, E. A. Hennig, U.S.A.
Long Horse, Anton Heida and Geo. Eyser, U.S.A., tied.
Side Horse, Anton Heida, U.S.A.
All-Round, Anton Heida, U.S.A.
Rope Climbing, George Eyser, U.S.A.
Flying Rings, Herman T. Glass, U.S.A.
Parallel Bars, George Eyser, U.S.A.
Horizontal Bars, Anton Heida, U.S.A.

1906

Team Gymnastics, Norway.
Five Events, 1st Class, Lavielle, France.
    2nd Class, Anastassaglous, Greece.
Six Events, 1st Class, Weber, Germany.
Rope Climb, D. Aliprantis, Greece.

1908

Team Gymnastics, Sweden
Individual Gymnastics, G. A. Braglia, Italy.

1912

Team Competition with Movements according to Swedish System, Sweden
Team Competition According to Special Conditions, Italy.
Team Competition with Free Choice of Movements and Apparatus, Norway.
Individual Competition, Alberto Braglia, Italy.

1920

Team Gymnastics, Italy.
Individual Gymnastics, G. Zampose, Italy.

1924

Team Gymnastics, Italy.
Long Horse, F. Kriz, U.S.A.
Side Horse, Jean Gounot, France.
Pommeled Horse, Wilhem, Switzerland.
All-Round, M. Stukelj, Jugoslavia.
Rope, Supcik, Czechoslovakia.
Rings, Donato Martino, Italy.
Parallel Bars, J. Guttinger, Switzerland.
Horizontal Bars, M. Stukelj, Jugoslavia.

1928

Team Gymnastics, Switzerland.
Side Horse, Haenggi, Switzerland.
Broad Horse Jump, Mack, Switzerland.
Rings, M. Stukelj, Jugoslavia.
Parallel Bars, Vacha, Czechoslovakia.
Horizontal Bars, Miez, Switzerland.
Final Standing Five Events, Miez, Switzerland.

WEIGHT-LIFTING

1896

Two Hands, V. Jensen, Denmark.
One Hand, L. Elliot, Great Britain.

1904

Lifting Bar Bell, P. Lakousis, Greece.
Dumbell Competition, O. C. Osthoff, U.S.A.

1906

Lifting Dumbbell Each Hand Separately, Steinbach, Austria.
Lifting Bar Bell Both Hands, D. Tofolas, Greece.

1920

Featherweight, F. DeHaes, Belgium.
Lightweight, A. Neyland, Esthonia.

1924

Featherweight, M. Gabetti, Italy.
Lightweight, Edmond Decottignies, France.
Middleweight, P. Galimberti, Italy.
Light-Heavyweight, Charles Rigoulet, France.
Heavyweight, J. Tonani, Italy.

1928

Featherweight, F. Andrysek, Austria.
Lightweight, K. Helbig, Germany, and H. Hass, Austria, tied.
Middleweight, F. Roger, France.
Light-Heavyweight, E. S. Nosseir, Egypt.
Heavyweight, J. Strassberger, Germany.

SHOOTING

1906

Any recognized Army Rifle, 300 meters, Standing or Kneeling, Richardet, Switzerland.
Gras Army Rifle, 200 Meters, Standing or Kneeling, Captain Moreaus, France.
Any Rifle, 300 Meters, Standing or Kneeling, Meyer de Stadelhofen, Switzerland.
International Team of Five, 300 Meters, Switzerland.
Gun Championship, Skattebo, Norway.
Gun Championship, Standing Position, Skattebo, Norway.
Gun Championship, Kneeling Position, Staeheli, Switzerland.
Gun Championship, Prone Position, Skattebo, Norway.
Any recognized Army Revolver, 20 Meters, Richardet, Switzerland.
Army Revolver, Design No. 1873, 20 Meters, Fouconnier, France
Any Revolver, 25 Meters, Lecoq, France.
Any Revolver, 50 Meters, G. Orthanidis, Greece.
Duelling Pistols, 20 Meters, Deliberate Aim, Captain Moreaux, France.
Duelling Pistols, 25 Meters, at Command, Skarlatos, Greece.
Sporting Shotgun, Clay Pigeons, Single Shot, Gerald Merlin, Great Britain.
Sporting Shotgun, Clay Pigeons, Double Shot, Signey Merlin, Great Britain.

1908

International Match, U.S.A.
300 Meters Team, Norway.

1000 Yards Individual, Col. J. K. Millner, G. B.
300 Meters Individual, A. Hilgerud, Norway.
Running Deer Shooting (110 Yards Team),
   Sweden.
110 Yards Individual, Double Shot, W. Winans,
   U.S.A.
110 Yards Individual, Single Shot, O. G. Swahn,
   Sweden.
Miniature Rifle Competition, Moving Target,
   W. Pimm, Great Britain.
Miniature Rifle Competition, Disappearing
   Target, W. E. Styles.
Team Competition, 50 and 100 Yards, Gt. Br.
Individual, 50 and 100 Yards, T. Plater, Gt. Br.
   REVOLVER AND PISTOL SHOOTING
Team Competition, 50 and 100 Yards, U.S.A.
Individual Competition, 50 Yards, P. Van
   Aesbrock, Belgium.

Clay Bird Shooting

Team Competition, Great Britain.
Individual Competition, W. H. Ewing, Canada.

1912

Army Rifle Team Competition, 200, 400, 500,
   and 600 Meters, U.S.A.
Individual Competition, 600 Meters, P. R.
   Colas, France.
Individual Competition, 300 Meters, A. Pro-
   kopp, Hungary.
Any Rifle Team Competition, 300 Meters,
   Sweden.
Individual Competition, 300 Meters, P. R.
   Colas, France.
Team Competition, Miniature Rifle Shooting,
   50 Meters, Great Britain.
Individual Competition, Miniature Rifle, 50
   Meters, F. S. Hird, U.S.A.
Team Competition, Miniature Rifle, 25 Meters,
   Sweden.
Individual Competition, Miniature Rifle, 25
   Meters, W. Carlberg, Sweden.
Team Competition, Revolver and Pistol, 50
   Meters, U.S.A.
Individual Competition, Revolver and Pistol,
   50 Meters, A. P. Lane, U.S.A.
Team Competition, Revolver and Pistol, 30
   Meters (Duel Shooting), Sweden.
Individual Competition, Revolver and Pistol,
   30 Meters (Duel Shooting), A. P. Lane,
   U.S.A.

Clay Bird Shooting

Team Competition, U.S.A.
Individual Competition, James R. Graham,
   U.S.A.

Running Deer Shooting

100 Meters, Single Shot
Team Competition, Sweden.
Individual Competition, Alfred G. A. Swahn,
   Sweden.

Running Deer Shooting

100 Meters, Double Shot
Individual Competition, Ake Lundeberg, Sweden.

1920

Trapshooting

Team Competition, U.S.A.
Individual Competition, Arie, U.S.A.

Rifle Shooting

Running Deer Shooting, Single Shot, Norway.
Running Deer Shooting, Double Shot, Norway.

Matches for Military Rifles

Team Match, 300 Meters, Standing, Denmark.
Individual Match, 300 Meters, Standing, Carl
   T. Osburn, U.S.A.
Team Match, 300 Meters, Prone Position,
   U.S.A.
Individual Match, 300 Meters, Prone Position,
   Lilloe Olsen, Norway.
Team Match, 600 Meters, Prone Position,
   U.S.A.
Individual Match, 600 Meters, Prone Position,
   Johansson, Sweden.
Team Match, 300 and 600 Meters, U.S.A.

Matches for Rifles of any Pattern

Team of Five Men, 300 Meters, U.S.A.
Any Rifle, Individual, Sgt. Morris Fisher,
   U.S.A.

Matches for Miniature Rifles

Team Match, 50 Meters, U.S.A.

Pistol and Revolver Shooting

Team Competition, 50 Meters, U.S.A.
Individual Competition, 50 Meters, Karl Fred-
   erick, U.S.A.
Thirty Meters Revolver Match, U.S.A.
Individual Revolver Match, Paraines, Brazil.

1924

Rifle, Individual, Morris Fisher, U.S.A.
Rifle, Team, U.S.A.
Miniature Rifle, Charles De Lisle, France.
Revolver, Individual, H. M. Baley, U.S.A.
Running Deer, Single Shot, Team, Norway.
Running Deer, Double Shot, Team, Great
   Britain.
Running Deer, Single Shot, J. K. Boles, U.S.A.
Running Deer, Double Shot, Individual, Lilloe
   Olsen, Norway.
Clay Pigeons, Team, U.S.A.
Clay Pigeons, Individual, Jules Halasy, Hun-
   gary.

Equestrian

1912

Military Team Competition, Sweden.
Military Individual Competition, Lt. A. Nord-
   lander, Sweden.
Prize Riding, Captain C. Bonde, Sweden.
Prize Riding, Individual Competition, Captain
   J. Cariou, France.
Prize Jumping, Team Competition, Sweden.

Vaulting Competition, Trooper Bonckaert, Belgium.
Jumping Competition, Lieut. Lequio, Italy.

1920

50 Kilometers Race, Lieut. Johansen, Norway.
20 Kilometers Race, Lieut. Misonna, Belgium.
Team and Individual Jumping Competition, Lieut. deMowne-, Sweden.
Individually-Trained Horse, Captain Lundblatt, Sweden.

1924

Individual Championship, Comprising 3 Tests, M. Van Der Woort, Holland.
Test 1—Horse Training, V. DeLinder, Sweden.
Test 2—Endurance, Sloan Doak, U.S.A.
Test 3—Obstacle Jump, M. Van Der Woort, Holland.
Individual Training Competitions, Hans Colenbrander, Holland.
Individual Obstacle Jump, Lieut. Gemusans, Switzerland.
Team Obstacle Jumping, Sweden.

1928

Individual Competition, Lieut. Mortanges, Holland.
Training Individual Competition, Capt. G. P. de Kruijff Jr., Holland.
Obstacle Jumping Competition, C. F. Freiherr von Langen, Germany.

FENCING

INDIVIDUAL FOILS

1904	Ramon Foust, Cuba.
1906	Dillon Cavanagh, France.
1912	Nedo Nadi, Italy.
1920	Nedo Nadi, Italy.
1924	Roger Ducret, France.
1928	Gaudin, France.

WOMEN

1924	Mrs. E. O. Osier, Denmark.
1928	Miss Mayer, Germany.

SINGLE STICKS

1904 A. V. Z. Post, Cuba.

TEAM FOILS

1904	Cuba.
1920	Italy.
1924	France.
1928	Italy.

INDIVIDUAL EPEE

1906	Comte de La Falaise, France.
1908	G. Alibert, France.
1912	P. Anspach, Belgium.
1920	M. Massard, France.
1924	H. Delporte, Belgium.
1928	Gaudin, France.

TEAM EPEE

1906	Germany.
1908	France.
1912	Belgium.
1920	Italy.
1924	France.
1928	Italy.

INDIVIDUAL SABRE

1904	M. De Diaz, Cuba.
1906	Georgiadis, Greece.
1908	E. Fuchs, Hungary.
1912	E. Fuchs, Hungary.
1920	Nedo Nadi, Italy.
1924	Alexandre Posta, Hungary.
1928	Tersztyanszky, Hungary.

TEAM SABRE

1906	Germany.
1908	Hungary.
1912	Hungary.
1920	Italy.
1924	Italy.
1928	Hungary.

THREE-CORNERED SABRE

1906 Casimir, Germany.

INDIVIDUAL SWORDS

1904 Ramon Foust, Cuba.

TENNIS

1904

Men's Singles, Beals C. Wright, U.S.A.
Men's Doubles, E. W. Leonard and Beals C. Wright, U.S.A.

1906

Men's Singles Championships, M. Decugis, France.
Men's Doubles Championships, M. Decugis and Germot, France.
Women's Singles Championships, Miss Semyriotou, Greece.
Mixed Doubles Championships, Mr. and Mrs. Decugis, France.

1908

Men's Singles, M. J. G. Ritchie, Great Britain.
Men's Doubles, G. W. Hillyard and R. F. Doherty, Great Britain.
Women's Singles, Mrs. Lambert Chambers, Great Britain.

1912

Men's Singles, C. L. Winslow, South Africa.
Men's Doubles, H. A. Kitson and C. Winslow, South Africa.
Women's Singles, Miss M. Broquedis, France.
Mixed Doubles, Miss D. Koring and H. Schomburgh, Germany.

1920

Men's Singles, Raymond, South Africa.
Women's Singles, Miss Lenglen, France.
Men's Doubles, Turnbull and Woosnam, Great Britain.
Mixed Doubles, M. Decugis and Miss Lenglen, France.
Women's Doubles, Mrs. McNair and Miss McKane, Great Britain.

1924

Men's Singles, Vincent Richards, U S.A.
Women's Singles, Miss Helen Wills, U.S.A.
Men's Doubles, Vincent Richards and F. T. Hunter, U.S.A.
Women's Doubles, Miss Helen Willis and Mrs. G. W. Wightman, U.S.A.
Mixed Doubles, Mrs. G. W. Wightman and R. N. Williams, U.S.A.

COVERED COURTS

1908

Men's Singles, A. W. Gore, Great Britain.
Men's Doubles, A. W. Gore and H. Roper Barrett, Great Britain.
Women's Singles, Miss G. Eastlake Smith, Great Britain.

1912

Men's Singles, A. H. Gobert, France.
Women's Singles, Mrs. E. M. Hannam, Great Britain.
Men's Doubles, A. H. Gobert and M. Germot, France.
Mixed Doubles, Mrs. E. M. Hannam and C. P. Dixon, Great Britain.

ROWING

EIGHT-OARED

1904 United States.
1908 Great Britain.
1912 Great Britain.
1920 United States.
1924 United States.
1928 United States.

SINGLE SCULLS

1904 Frank B. Greer, U.S.A.
1908 H. T. Blackstaffe, Great Britain.
1912 W. D. Kinnear, Great Britain.
1920 J. B. Kelly, U.S.A.
1924 Jack Beresford, Jr., Great Britain.
1928 Pearce, Australia.

DOUBLE SCULLS

1904 United States.
1908 J. R. K. Fenning and G. L. Thomson, Great Britain.
1920 J. B. Kelly and Paul V. Costello, U.S.A.
1924 J. B. Kelly and Paul V. Costello, U.S.A.
1928 Paul V. Costello and Charles J. McIlvaine, U.S.A.

FOURS WITH COXSWAIN

1906 Italy.
1912 Germany.
1920 Switzerland.
1924 Switzerland.
1928 Italy.

FOUR-OARED WITHOUT COXSWAIN

1904 United States.
1908 Great Britain.
1924 Great Britain.
1928 Switzerland.

PAIR OARS WITH COXSWAIN

1906 Italy (1600 Meters).
1906 Italy (1000 Meters).
1920 E. Olgeni and G. Scatturin, Italy.
1924 M. Candevear and J. Felber, Switzerland.
1928 Switzerland.

PAIR-OARED WITHOUT COXSWAIN

1904 United States.
1908 Great Britain.
1924 W. H. Rosingh and A. C. Reynen, Holland.
1928 Germany.

1906

Canoe Race, Singles, Delaplane, France.

1912

Four-Oared, Inriggers, Denmark.

YACHTING

1908

12 Meters Class, Hera, Great Britain.
8 Meters Class, Cobweb, Great Britain.
7 Meters Class, Heroine, Great Britain.
6 Meters Class, Dormy, Great Britain.

1912

12 Meters Class, Magda IX, Norway.
10 Meters Class, Kitty, Sweden.
8 Meters Class, Taifun, Norway.
6 Meters Class, Mac Murche, France.

1920

12 Meters Class (new), Heira II, Norway.
12 Meters Class (old), Atalanta, Norway.
10 Meters Class (new), Mosk II, Norway.
10 Meters Class (old), Eleda, Norway.
8 Meters Class (new), Sildra, Norway.
8 Meters Class (old), Ierne, Norway.
7 Meters Class (old), Ancora, Great Britain.
6 Meters Class (new), Jo, Norway.
6 Meters Class (old), Edelweiss, Belgium.
40 Square Feet, Sif, Sweden.
30 Square feet, Kullan, Sweden.
640-Class Yacht, Oranje, Holland.
18 Ft. Class, Brat, Great Britain.
12 Ft. Class, Boreas, Holland and Beatriss III Holland, tied.

1924

One Design Class, Single handed, Belgium.
6 Meter Class, Norway.
8 Meter Class, Norway.

1928

8 Meter Class, France.
6 Meter Class, Norway.
Dinghy Class, Sweden.

Winter Sports

1924

Speed Skating Glas Thunberg, Finland.
500 Meters Skating, Charles Jewtraw, U.S.A.
1500 Meters Skating, Glas Thunberg, Finland.
5000 Meters Skating, Glas Thunberg, Finland.
10000 Meters Skating, Julien Skutnabb, Finland.
Figure Skating, Women, Mrs. H. Szabo, Austria.
Figure Skating, Men Gillis Grafstrom, Sweden.
Figure Skating, Couples, Mrs. Englemann and T. Berger, Austria.

1928

500 Meters Skating, Glas Thunberg, Finland and Bernt Evensen, Norway, tied.
1500 Meters Skating, Glas Thunberg, Finland.
5000 Meters Skating, Ivar Ballengrund, Norway.
10000 Meters Skating, Irving Jaffee made best time, but on account of thawing of ice, race was cancelled
Figure Skating, Women, Miss Sonja Henie, Norway.

Figure Skating, Men, Gillis Grafstrom, Sweden.
Figure Skating, Couples, Miss Andree Jolly and Pierre Brunet, France.
Ski, (31 miles), Pete Hedlund, Sweden.
Ski (12 miles), Johann Gottensbraaten Norway.
Ski Jump, Alfred Anderson, Norway.
Skiing, Combined, J Gottensbraaten, Norway.
Bobsleigh, U.S.A (Capt. Fiske).
Skeleton, John Heaton, U.S.A.
Ice Hockey, Canada.
Military Ski by Teams, Norway.

1932

500 meters speed-skating, Jack Shea, U.S.A.
1500 meters speed-skating, Jack Shea, U.S.A.
5000 meters speed skating, Irving Jaffee, U.S.A.
10,000 meters speed-skating, Irving Jaffee, U.S.A.
*Women's figure-skating, Sonja Henie, Norway.
Men's figure-skating, Karl Schaefer, Austria.
*Pair figure-skating, M. and Mme. Pierre Brunot, France.
*Combined skiing, Johan Grottumsbraaten, Norway.
18-kilometer ski run , Sven Utterstrom, Sweden.
50-kilometer ski run, Veli Saarinen, Finland.
Ski-jump, Berger Ruud, Norway.
*Hockey, Canada.
Two-man bobsled, J. Hubert Stevens, U.S.A, driver.
*Four-man bobsled, William I. Fiske, U.S.A., driver
Team (unofficial), U.S.A.
*Retained title.

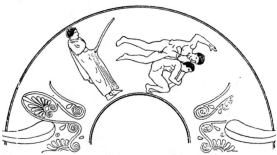

Wrestling Scene

What is known to moderns as the "flying-mare" was a favorite "hold" of ancient Grecian wrestlers. The above scene is taken from a cylix, now in the British Museum. It shows two Grecian wrestlers practicing under the watchful eye of their trainer who stands ready to wield the rod at any infraction of the rules.

OFFICIAL WORLD'S TRACK AND FIELD RECORDS

(Accepted by the International Amateur Athletic Federation, May, 1930)

RUNNING — YARD BASIS

EVENT	RECORD	HOLDER AND NATION	WHERE MADE	DATE
100 yards	9 5s	Eddie Tolan, United States	Evanston, Ill., U.S.A.	May 25, 1929
220 yards	20.6s	Roland A. Locke, United States	Lincoln, Neb., U.S.A.	May 1, 1926
300 yards	30.6s	B. J. Wefers, United States	New York, N. Y., U.S.A.	Sept. 26, 1896
440 yards	47.4s	G. M. Butler, Great Britain	London, England	June 26, 1926
		J. E. Meredith, United States	Cambridge, Mass., U.S.A.	May 27, 1916
600 yards	1m. 10.4s	D. G. A. Lowe, Great Britain	London, England	June 26, 1926
880 yards	1m. 51.6s	Dr. Otto Peltzer, Germany	London, England	July 3, 1926
1000 yards	2m. 11.2s	C. Ellis, Great Britain	London, England	Sept. 7, 1929
1320 yards	3m. 2.8s	T. P. Conneff, United States	New York, N. Y., U.S.A.	Aug. 21, 1895
1 mile	4m. 10.4s	Paavo Nurmi, Finland	Stockholm, Sweden	Aug. 23, 1923
2 miles	9m. 1.4s	Edwin Wide, Sweden	Charlottenburg, Germany	Sept. 12, 1926
3 miles	14m. 11.2s	Paavo Nurmi, Finland	Stockholm, Sweden	Aug. 24, 1923
4 miles	19m. 15.6s	Paavo Nurmi, Finland	Kuopio, Finland	Oct. 1, 1924
5 miles	24m. 6.2s	Paavo Nurmi, Finland	Kuopio, Finland	Oct. 1, 1924
6 miles	29m. 59.4s	Alfred E. Shrubb, Great Britain	Glasgow, Scotland	Nov. 5, 1904
7 miles	35m. 4.6s	Alfred E. Shrubb, Great Britain	Glasgow, Scotland	Nov. 5, 1904
8 miles	40m. 16s	Alfred E. Shrubb, Great Britain	Glasgow, Scotland	Nov. 5, 1904
9 miles	45m. 27.6s	Alfred E. Shrubb, Great Britain	Glasgow, Scotland	Nov. 5, 1904
10 miles	50m. 15s	Paavo Nurmi, Finland	Berlin, Germany	Oct. 7, 1928
15 miles	1h. 20m. 4.4s	F. Appleby, Great Britain	London, England	July 21, 1902
20 miles	1h. 51m. 54s	G. Crossland, Great Britain	London, England	Sept. 22, 1894
25 miles	2h. 29m. 29.4s	H. Green, Great Britain	London, England	May 12, 1913
1 hour	11 miles 1,648 yds.	Paavo Nurmi, Finland	Berlin, Germany	Oct. 7, 1928
2 hours	20 miles 952 yds.	H. Green, Great Britain	London, England	May 12, 1913

RUNNING — METRIC DISTANCES

EVENT	RECORD	HOLDER AND NATION	WHERE MADE	DATE
100 meters	10.4s	Charles W. Paddock, United States	Redlands, Calif., U.S.A.	Apr. 23, 1921
		Eddie Tolan, United States	Copenhagen, Denmark	Aug. 28, 1929
200 meters	20.6s	Roland A. Locke, United States	Lincoln, Neb., U.S.A.	May 1, 1926
300 meters	33.2s	Charles W. Paddock, United States	Redlands, Calif., U.S.A.	Apr. 23, 1921
400 meters	47s	Emerson Spencer, United States	Palo Alto, Calif., U.S.A.	May 12, 1928
500 meters	1m. 3s	E. Tavenari, Italy	Budapest, Hungary	June 14, 1928
800 meters	1m. 50.6s	S. Martin, France	Paris, France	July 15, 1929
1000 meters	2m. 25.8s	Dr. Otto Peltzer, Germany	Paris, France	Sept. 18, 1927
1500 meters	3m. 51s	Dr. Otto Peltzer, Germany	Charlottenburg, Germany	Sept. 9, 1926
2000 meters	5m. 23.4s	E. Borg (Purje), Finland	Viborg, Finland	Aug. 13, 1927
3000 meters	8m. 20.4s	Paavo Nurmi, Finland	Stockholm, Sweden	July 19, 1924
5000 meters	14m. 28.2s	Paavo Nurmi, Finland	Helsinki, Finland	June 19, 1924
10000 meters	30m. 6.2s	Paavo Nurmi, Finland	Kuopio, Finland	Aug. 31, 1924
15000 meters	46m. 49.6s	Paavo Nurmi, Finland	Berlin, Germany	Oct. 7, 1928

EVENT	RECORD	HOLDER AND NATION	WHERE MADE		DATE
20000 meters	1h. 6m. 29s	V. Sipila, Finland	Stockholm	Sweden	June 19, 1925
25000 meters	1h. 23m. 45.8s	E. Harper, Great Britain	Berlin	Germany	Aug. 25, 1929
30000 meters	1h. 43m. 7.8s	V. Sipila, Finland	Tampere	Finland	Sept 16, 1928
1 hour	19,210 meters	Paavo Nurmi, Finland	Berlin	Germany	Oct. 7, 1928
2 hours	33,056 meters	H. Green, Great Britain	London	England	May 12, 1913

WALKING

EVENT	RECORD	HOLDER AND NATION	WHERE MADE		DATE
1 mile	6m. 25 8s	G. H. Goulding, Canada	Montreal	Canada	June 4, 1910
2 miles	13m. 11 4s	G. E. Larner, Great Britain	London	England	July 13, 1904
3 miles	20m. 25.8s	G. E. Larner, Great Britain	London	England	Aug. 19, 1905
4 miles	27m. 14s	G. E. Larner, Great Britain	London	England	Aug. 19, 1905
5 miles	36m. 0.2s	G. E. Larner, Great Britain	London	England	Sept. 30, 1905
6 miles	43m. 26 2s	G. E. Larner, Great Britain	London	England	Sept. 30, 1905
7 miles	50m. 40.8s	G. H. Goulding, Canada	New York, N. Y.	U.S.A.	Oct. 23, 1915
8 miles	58m. 18.4s	G. E. Larner, Great Britain	London	England	Sept. 30, 1905
9 miles	1h. 7m. 37.8s	G. E. Larner, Great Britain	London	England	July 17, 1908
10 miles	1h. 15m. 57 4s	G. E. Larner, Great Britain	London	England	July 17, 1908
15 miles	1h. 59m. 12.6s	H. V. L. Ross, Great Britain	Liverpool	England	May 20, 1911
20 miles	2h. 47m. 52s	T. Griffith, Great Britain	London	England	Dec. 3, 1870
25 miles	3h. 37m. 6 8s	S. C. A. Schofield, Great Britain	Glasgow	Scotland	May 20, 1911
1 hour	8 miles 438 yds	G. E. Larner, Great Britain	London	England	Sept. 30, 1905
2 hours	15 miles 128 yds	H. V. L. Ross, Great Britain	Liverpool	England	May 20, 1911

WALKING — METRIC DISTANCES

EVENT	RECORD	HOLDER AND NATION	WHERE MADE		DATE
3000 meters	12m. 53.8s	G. Rasmussen, Denmark	Copenhagen	Denmark	July 7, 1918
5000 meters	21m. 59.8s	G. Rasmussen, Denmark	Copenhagen	Denmark	July 6, 1918
10000 meters	45m. 26.4s	G. Rasmussen, Denmark	Copenhagen	Denmark	Aug. 18, 1918
15000 meters	1h. 10m. 23s	G. Rasmussen, Denmark	Copenhagen	Denmark	May 9, 1918
20000 meters	1h. 37m. 42 2s	D. Pavesi, Italy	Milan	Italy	Oct. 23, 1927
25000 meters	2h. 5m. 12.2s	A. Schwab, Switzerland	Berlin	Germany	Apr. 10, 1927
1 hour	13,275 meters	G. E. Larner, Great Britain	London	England	Sept. 30, 1905
2 hours	24,256 meters	H. V. L. Ross, Great Britain	Liverpool	England	May 20, 1911

HURDLES (10 HURDLES)

EVENT	HOLDER AND NATION	WHERE MADE		DATE
120 yds. (3ft. 6in. hdles.) 14 4s	E. J. Thomson, Canada	Philadelphia, Pa.	U.S.A.	May 29, 1920
	E. Wennstrom, Sweden	Stockholm	Sweden	Aug. 25, 1929
220 yds. (2ft. 6in. hdles) 23s	C. R. Brookins, United States	Ames, Iowa	U.S.A.	May 17, 1924
440 yds. (3ft. hdles.) 52 6s	John A. Gibson, United States	Lincoln, Neb.	U.S.A.	July 2, 1927

HURDLES — METRIC DISTANCES (10 HURDLES)

EVENT	HOLDER AND NATION	WHERE MADE		DATE
110 mtrs. (3ft. 6in. hdles.) 14.4s	E. Wennstrom, Sweden	Stockholm	Sweden	Aug. 25, 1929
200 mtrs. (2ft. 6in. hdles.) 23s	C. R. Brookins, United States	Ames, Iowa	U.S.A.	May 17, 1924
400 mtrs. (3ft. hdles.) 52s	F. Morgan Taylor, United States	Philadelphia, Pa.	U.S.A.	July 4, 1928

Official World's Track and Field Records (Continued)

Relay Races

EVENT	RECORD	HOLDER AND NATION		WHERE MADE		DATE
440 yards (4x110) ..	41s...	Newark A.C. (C. Bowman, J. Currie, J. Pappas, H. H Cumming Jr.).....	United States..	Lincoln, Neb. . .	U.S.A.	July 4, 1927
880 yards (4x220) ..	1m. 25.8s	Univ. of Southern California (C. E Borah, E. House, H Smith, W Lewis)	United States .	Los Angeles, Calif.	U.S.A.	May 14, 1927
1 mile (4x440)	3m. 13 4s	U. S. A. Team (G. Baird, F. M. Taylor, R. J Barbuti, E. Spencer)....	United States..	London . . .	England . .	Aug 11, 1928
2 miles (4x880)..	7m. 41 4s	Boston A.A (S. H. Martin, C. Sansone, L. Welch, L. Hahn)	United States	Philadelphia, Pa	U.S.A.	July 6, 1928
4 miles (4x1 mile) ..	17m. 21 4s	Illinois A C. (E. Krogh, Ray Watson, Ray Buker, Joie Ray)....	United States.	Chicago, Ill. .	U S.A....	June 23, 1923

Relay Races — Metric Distances

EVENT	RECORD	HOLDER AND NATION		WHERE MADE		DATE
400 meters (4x100)..	40.8s. ...	German National Team—(Jonath, Corts, Houben, Kornig)	Germany	Berlin	Germany ..	Sept. 2, 1928
		Sp. C. Charlottenburg (Kornig, Grosser, Nathan, H. Schlosske)	Germany ..	Breslau ...	Germany..	July 22, 1929
800 meters (4x200)	1m 25.8s	Univ. of Southern California (C. E. Borah, E. House, H. Smith, W. Lewis) ...	United States	Los Angeles, Calif ..	U S.A.	May 14, 1927
1600 meters (4x400)	3 m 13.4s	U. S. A. Team (G. Baird, F, M. Taylor, R. J. Barbuti, E. Spencer)	United States	London	England	Aug 11, 1928
3200 meters (4x800)	7m. 41.4s..	Boston A. A. (S. H. Martin, C. Sansone, L. Welch, L. Hahn)......	United States .	Philadelphia, Pa. .	U.S.A. . .	July 6, 1926
6000 meters (4x1500)	16m 11.4s	Turun Urheiluitto, Ab (Levendahl, Katz, Koivunalho, Nurmi)......	Finland ..	Viborg...........	Finland	July 17, 1926

JUMPING

EVENT	RECORD	HOLDER AND NATION	WHERE MADE	DATE
Standing high jump	5ft. 5 3-4in. (167cm)	Leo Goehring, United States	New York, N. Y., U.S.A.	June 14, 1913
Running high jump	6ft. 8 1-4in. (203cm)	H. M. Osborn, United States	Urbana, Ill., U.S.A.	May 27, 1924
Standing broad jump	11ft. 4 7-8in. (347cm)	R. C. Ewry, United States	St. Louis, Mo., U.S.A.	Aug. 29, 1904
Running broad jump	26ft. 1-8in. (793cm)	S. Cator, Haiti	Paris, France	Sept. 9, 1928
Run, hop, step and jump	50ft. 11 1-4in. (15.52m)	A. W. Winter, Australia	Paris, France	July 12, 1924
Pole vault	14ft. 1 1-2in. (430cm)	Lee Barnes, United States	Fresno, Calif., U.S.A.	Apr. 28, 1928

WEIGHTS

EVENT	RECORD	HOLDER AND NATION	WHERE MADE	DATE
16lb shop put.	52ft. 7 1-2in (16 1-2.04m)	E. Hirschfeld, Germany	Bochum, Germany	Aug. 26, 1928
Both hands — Right, 50ft. 6in (15.39m) Left, 41ft 41-2in. (12.61m) }	91ft. 10 1-2 in. (28m)	Ralph Rose, United States	Oakland, Calif., U.S.A.	June 2, 1912
16-lb. hammer throw	189ft. 6 1-2in. (57.77m)	P. J. Ryan, United States	New York, N. Y., U.S.A.	Aug 17, 1913
56-lb. weight throw	40ft. 6 3-8in. (12.35m)	M. J. McGrath, United States	Montreal, Canada	Sept. 23, 1911

DISCUS THROW

EVENT	RECORD	HOLDER AND NATION	WHERE MADE	DATE
Best hand	163ft. 8 3-4in. (49.90m)	Eric C. W. Krenz, United States	Palo Alto, Calif. U.S.A.	Mar. 9, 1929
Both hands Right, 149ft 6⅝in (45 57m) Left, 146ft. 2⅜in (44 56m) }	295ft. 8 1-2in. (90.13m)	E. Nicklander, Finland	Helsinki, Finland	July 20, 1913

JAVELIN THROW

EVENT	RECORD	HOLDER AND NATION	WHERE MADE	DATE
Best hand	232ft. 11 5-8in. (71.01m)	E. H. Lundquist, Sweden	Stockholm, Sweden	Aug. 15, 1928
Both hands {Right Left }	374ft. 11 3-8in. (114 28m)	Y. Hackner, Sweden	Karlskoga, Sweden	Sept. 30, 1917

DECATHLON

EVENT	RECORD	HOLDER AND NATION	WHERE MADE	DATE
8053.290 points		Paavo Yrjola, Finland.	Amsterdam, Holland	Aug. 3-4, 1928

UNOFFICIAL WORLD'S RECORDS

(The following marks excell present world's records but have not been recognized officially.)

EVENT	RECORD	HOLDER AND NATION	WHERE MADE	DATE
440 yard run	46.4s	Ben Eastman, U.S.A.	Palo Alto, Calif., U.S.A.	Mar. 26, 1932
880 yard run	1m. 51.3s	Ben Eastman, U.S.A.	Palo Alto, Calif., U.S.A.	Apr. 9, 1932
1 mile run	4m. 9.4s	Jules Ladoumegue, France.	Paris, France	June 1931
2 mile run	8m. 59 6s	Paavo Nurmi, Finland	Helsingfors, Finland	July 1931
Shot put *	52ft. 8 3-8in	Leo Sexton, U.S.A.	New York, N. Y., U. S. A.	Feb. 17, 1932
Running high jump*	6ft. 8 1-2in.	George Spitz, U.S.A.	Boston, Mass., U.S.A.	Feb. 13, 1932
Running broad jump	26ft. 2 1-8in.	Chuhei Nambu, Japan	Tokio, Japan	Oct. 27, 1931
Hop, step, jump	51ft. 1 1-4in.	Mikio Oda, Japan	Tokio, Japan	Oct. 27, 1931

*Indoors.

WORLD'S RECORDS RECOMMENDED FOR APPROVAL

TRACK AND FIELD RECORDS

S. Stankovits, in charge of the permanent Bureau of World's Records at Budapest, will recommend the following records for adoption by the International Amateur Athletic Federation, when it meets at Los Angeles in July, 1932.

Event	Record	Holder and Nation	Where Made	Date Made
100 yds. run	9.4s.	Frank Wykoff, United States	Los Angeles, Calif.	May 10, 1930
6 miles run	29m. 36.4s.	Paavo Nurmi, Finland	London, England	June 9, 1930
1000 mtrs. run	2m. 23 6s	Jules Ladoumegue, France	Paris, France	Oct. 19, 1930
1500 mtrs. run	3m. 49.2s.	Jules Ladoumegue, France	Paris, France	Oct. 5, 1930
20000 mtrs. run	1h. 4m. 38.4s.	Paavo Nurmi, Finland	Stockholm, Sweden	Sept. 3, 1930
25000 mtrs. run	1h. 22m. 28.8s.	Martti Marttelin, Finland	Viipuri, Finland	Sept. 14, 1930
120 yds hurdles	14.4s	Steve Anderson, United States	Pittsburgh, Pa.	Aug. 23, 1930
25000 mtrs. walk	2h 3m. 49s	Armando Valente, Italy	Paris, France	Sept. 28, 1930
2 hours walk	24275m. (15 miles 147 yds.)	Armando Valente, Italy	Paris, France	Sept. 28, 1930
Discus throw	169ft 8 7.8in. (51.73m.)	Paul Jessup, United States	Pittsburgh, Pa.	Aug. 23, 1930
Javelin throw	72.93m. (239ft. 3 1-4in.)	Matti Jarvinen, Finland	Viipuri, Finland	Sept. 14, 1930
Decathlon	8255 475 pts.	Akilles Jarvinen, Finland	Viipuri, Finland	July 20, 1930

SWIMMING RECORDS (MEN)

The Amateur Athletic Union of the United States has submitted to the International Amateur Swimming Federation the following American records for approval as world's records. Dr. Leo Donath, Secretary of the I.A.S.F., has accepted them subject to the approval of the Federation when it meets at Los Angeles in August, 1932.

Event	Record	Length of Course	Holder	Where Made	Date Made
880 yds. free style	10m 20 2-5s.	55 yds.	Clarence Crabbe	Long Beach, Calif.	July 6, 1930
150 yds. back stroke	1m. 38s.	25 yds	George H. Kojac	Cambridge, Mass.	Mar. 29, 1930
200 mtrs. back stroke	2m. 32 1-5s	25 yds	George H. Kojac	New Haven, Conn.	June 16, 1930

SWIMMING RECORDS (WOMEN)

Event	Record	Length of Course	Holder	Where Made	Date Made
100 yds. free style	1m. 4-5s.	25 yds	Helene Madison	Miami Beach, Fla.	Mar. 13, 1930
100 mtrs. free style	1m. 8s.	25 yds	Helene Madison	Miami Beach, Fla.	Mar. 14, 1930
150 yds. free style	1m. 40 2-5s	25 yds	Helene Madison	St. Augustine, Fla.	Mar. 6, 1930
150 yds. free style	1m. 43 4-5s.	25 yds	Catherine Ames	Cliffwood Beach, N. J.	Aug. 2, 1930
200 mtrs. free style.	2m. 34 3-5s.	25 yds	Helene Madison	St. Augustine, Fla	Mar. 6, 1930
220 yds. free style.	2m. 35s	25 yds.	Helene Madison	Miami Beach, Fla.	Mar. 18, 1930
300 yds. free style.	3m. 39s	25 yds.	Helene Madison	Seattle, Wash.	June 17, 1930
300 yds. free style.	3m. 41 3-5s	25 yds.	Helene Madison	Seattle, Wash.	Apr. 4, 1930
300 yds. free style	3m. 49s	25 yds	Josephine McKim	Miami Beach, Fla.	Mar. 14, 1930
300 mtrs. free style	3m. 59 5-10s	25 yds	Helene Madison	Seattle, Wash.	June 17, 1930
440 yds. free style	5m 39 2-5s.	25 yds.	Helene Madison	Long Beach, Calif.	July 4, 1930
500 yds. free style	6m. 16 2-5s	25 yds	Helene Madison	Miami Beach, Fla.	Mar. 16, 1930
880 yds. free style .	11m 41 1-5s.	55 yds	Helene Madison	Long Beach, Calif.	July 6, 1930
1 mile free style.	24m. 34 3-5s	55 yds.	Helene Madison	Long Beach, Calif.	July 3, 1930
200 mtrs. back stroke.	2m. 58 1-5s.	25 yds	Eleanor Holm	New York City	Mar. 1, 1930
200 mtrs back stroke	2m. 58 4-5s	25 yds	Eleanor Holm	Buffalo, N. Y.	Feb. 1, 1930

WORLD'S RECORDS TO BE SUBMITTED FOR ADOPTION

The following American track and swimming records will be submitted by the Amateur Athletic Union of the United States for adoption by the International Amateur Athletic Federation and the International Amateur Swimming Federation.

TRACK AND FIELD RECORDS (MEN)

Event	Record	Holder	Where Made	Date Made
440 yds. run	47.4s	Ben Eastman	Los Angeles, Calif.	May 16, 1931
440 yds. run	47.4s	Victor E. Williams	Philadelphia, Pa.	May 30, 1931
120 yds. hurdles (3ft. 6in. hdles.)	14.2s	Percy Beard	Lincoln, Neb.	July 4, 1931
400 mtrs. relay (4x100)	40.8s	Univ. of So. California (R. Delby, M. Maurer, M. Guyer, F. Wykoff)	Fresno, Calif.	May 9, 1931
440 yds. relay (4x110)	40.8s	Univ. of So. California (R. Delby, M. Maurer, M. Guyer, F. Wykoff)	Fresno, Calif.	May 9, 1931
1600 mtrs. relay (4x400)	3m. 12.6s	Stanford Univ. (M. Shove, A. A. Hables, L. I. Hables, B. Eastman)	Fresno, Calif.	May 8, 1931
1 mile relay (4x440)	3m. 12.6s	Stanford Univ. (M. Shove, A. A. Hables, L. I. Hables, B. Eastman)	Fresno, Calif.	May 8, 1931

TRACK AND FIELD RECORDS (WOMEN)

Event	Record	Holder	Where Made	Date Made
80 mtrs. run	9.9s	Stella Walsh	Cleveland, Ohio	July 5, 1931
80 mtrs. hurdles	12s	Mildred Didrikson	Jersey City, N. J.	July 25, 1931

SWIMMING RECORDS (MEN)

Distance	Time	Length of Course	Holder	Where Made	Date Made
200 mtrs. breast stroke	2m. 44.6s	25 yds	Leonard Spence	Chicago, Ill.	Apr. 2, 1931
800 mtrs. relay	9m 21.8s	55 yds	Hollywood A. C. (A. Clapp, Manuella Kalili, F. Boothe, Mai Kalili)	Honolulu, T.H.	July 15, 1931

SWIMMING RECORDS (WOMEN)

Distance	Time	Length of Course	Holder	Where Made	Date Made
100 yds. free style	60s	25 yds	Helene Madison	Boston, Mass.	Apr. 20, 1931
100 mtrs. free style	1m. 6.6s	25 yds	Helene Madison	Boston, Mass.	Apr. 20, 1931
220 yds. free style	2m. 34.8s	25 yds	Helene Madison	Seattle, Wash.	May 15, 1931
400 mtrs. free style	5m. 31s	25 yds	Helene Madison	Seattle, Wash.	Feb. 3, 1931
440 yds. free style	5m. 31s	25 yds	Helene Madison	Seattle, Wash.	Feb. 3, 1931
500 mtrs. free style	7m. 12s	25 yds	Helene Madison	Detroit, Mich.	Apr. 25, 1931
1000 yds. free style	13m 23.8s	55 yds	Helene Madison	New York City	July 17, 1931
1000 mtrs. free style	14m. 44.8s	55 yds	Helene Madison	New York City	July 19, 1931
1500 mtrs. free style	23m. 17.2s	55 yds	Helene Madison	New York City	July 15, 1931

WORLD'S SWIMMING RECORDS (MEN)

(Accepted by the International Amateur Swimming Federation to June 1, 1930.)

FREE STYLE

DISTANCE	TIME	LENGTH OF COURSE	HOLDER AND NATION	WHERE MADE	DATE MADE
100 yards	51s	25 yards	John Weissmuller, United States	Ann Arbor, Mich.	June 5, 1927
150 yards	1m. 25s	25 yards	Walter Laufer, United States	Chicago, Ill.	Mar. 2, 1929
220 yards	2m. 9s	25 yards	John Weissmuller, United States	Ann Arbor, Mich.	June 5, 1927
300 yards	3m. 7 4-5s	25 yards	John Weissmuller, United States	Chicago, Ill.	June 17, 1927
440 yards	4m. 52s	110 yards	John Weissmuller, United States	Honolulu, T.H.	Aug. 25, 1927
500 yards	5m. 31 2-5s	25 yards	Arne Borg, Sweden	Detroit, Mich	Jan. 30, 1926
880 yards	10m. 22 1-5s	110 yards	John Weissmuller, United States	Honolulu, T.H	July 27, 1927
1000 yards	12m. 16 8s	50 meters	Arne Borg, Sweden	Gothenburg	Sept. 3, 1924
1 mile	21m. 41.3s	50 meters	Arne Borg, Sweden	Gothenburg	Aug. 12, 1925
100 meters	57 2-5s	25 yards	John Weissmuller, United States	Miami, Fla	Feb. 17, 1924
200 meters	2m. 8s	25 yards	John Weissmuller, United States	Ann Arbor, Mich.	June 5, 1927
300 meters	3m. 33.5s	25 yards	Arne Borg, Sweden	Stockholm	Oct. 11, 1926
400 meters	4m. 50.3s	25 yards	Arne Borg, Sweden	Stockholm	Sept. 11, 1925
500 meters	6m. 8.4s	25 yards	Arne Borg, Sweden	Stockholm	Sept. 11, 1925
1000 meters	13m. 4.2s	50 meters	Arne Borg, Sweden	Oslo	Aug. 18, 1925
1500 meters	19m. 7.2s	50 meters	Arne Borg, Sweden	Bologna	Sept. 2, 1927

BREAST STROKE

DISTANCE	TIME	LENGTH OF COURSE	HOLDER AND NATION	WHERE MADE	DATE MADE
200 yards	2m. 31 4-5s	25 yards	Walter Spence, United States	Brooklyn, N.Y.	Mar. 19, 1927
100 meters	1m. 14s	25 yards	Walter Spence, United States	New York City	Oct. 28, 1927
200 meters	2m. 45s	25 meters	Y. Tsuruta, Japan	Kyoto	July 27, 1929
400 yards	5m. 50 1-5s	25 yards	Erich Rademacher, Germany	New Haven, Conn.	Mar. 9, 1926
500 meters	7m. 40.8s	25 yards	Erich Rademacher, Germany	Lepzig	Apr. 4, 1925

BACK STROKE

DISTANCE	TIME	LENGTH OF COURSE	HOLDER AND NATION	WHERE MADE	DATE MADE
150 yards	1m. 38.4s	25 yards	George Kojac, United States	St. Louis, Mo.	Mar 30, 1929
100 meters	1m. 9 3-5s	50 yards	George Kojac, United States.	Detroit, Mich.	June 23, 1928
200 meters	2m. 37.8s	50 meters	Toshio Iriye, Japan	Tamagawa	Oct. 14, 1928
400 meters	5m. 42s	25 meters	Toshio Iriye, Japan	Wakayama	Sept. 30, 1928

WORLD'S SWIMMING RECORDS (WOMEN)

FREE STYLE

DISTANCE	TIME	LENGTH OF COURSE	HOLDER AND NATION	WHERE MADE	DATE MADE
100 yards	60.9s	25 yards	Ethel Lackie, United States	Philadelphia, Pa.	Mar. 8, 1926
150 yards	1m. 45s	25 yards	Gertrude Ederle, United States	Bermuda	Oct. 7, 1922
220 yards	2m. 40 3-5s	25 yards	Martha Norelius, United States	Miami, Fla.	Feb. 28, 1926
300 yards	3m. 58.4s	25 yards	Gertrude Ederle, United States	Brighton Beach	Sept. 4, 1922
440 yards	5m. 47.4s	55 yards	Josephine McKim, United States	Honolulu, T.H.	Aug. 8, 1929
500 yards	6m. 32s	55 yards	Martha Norelius, United States	Buffalo, N.Y.	Feb. 5, 1927
880 yards	12m. 38s	55 yards	Josephine McKim, United States	Honolulu, T.H.	Aug. 10, 1929
1000 yards	13m. 39 2-5s	55 yards	Martha Norelius, United States	Massapequa, N.Y.	July 28, 1927
1 mile	24m. 49s	50 meters	Josephine McKim, United States	New York City	Feb. 7, 1928
100 meters	1m. 9.8s	55 yards	Albina Osipowich, United States	San Francisco, Calif.	Aug. 25, 1929
200 meters	2m. 40 3-5s	25 yards	Martha Norelius, United States	Miami, Fla.	Feb. 28, 1926
300 meters	4m. 8.3s	1-3 meters	Martha Norelius, United States	Vienna	Aug. 30, 1928
400 meters	5m. 39 3s	1-3 meters	Martha Norelius, United States	Vienna	Aug. 27, 1928
500 meters	7m 18s	25 meters	Marie Braun, Holland	Bruges	Mar. 23, 1930
1000 meters	13m. 39 2-5s	55 yards	Martha Norelius, United States	Massapequa, N.Y.	July 28, 1927
1500 meters	23m. 44 3-5s	55 yards	Martha Norelius, United States	Massapequa, N.Y.	July 28, 1927

BREAST STROKE

DISTANCE	TIME	LENGTH OF COURSE	HOLDER AND NATION	WHERE MADE	DATE MADE
200 yards	2m. 57.8s	25 meters	Hilda Schrader, Germany	Magdeburg	Dec. 17, 1929
100 meters	1m 26 3s	25 yards	Lotte Muhe, Germany	Magdeburg	June 9, 1928
200 meters	3m 11 2-5s	50 meters	Lotte Muhe, Germany	Berlin	July 15, 1928
400 meters	6m. 45.6s	25 meters	Marie Baron, Holland	Brussels	Nov. 24, 1928

BACK STROKE

DISTANCE	TIME	LENGTH OF COURSE	HOLDER AND NATION	WHERE MADE	DATE MADE
150 yards	1m 56.2s	25 yards	M. J. Cooper, Great Britain	London, Eng.	Apr. 29, 1930
100 meters	1m. 21s	25 meters	Marie Braun, Holland	Gravenhage	Nov. 27, 1929
200 meters	2m. 59.2s	25 meters	Marie Braun, Holland	Brussels	Nov. 24, 1928
400 meters	6m. 16.8s	25 meters	Marie Braun, Holland	Paris	Dec. 23, 1928

WOMEN'S WORLD TRACK AND FIELD RECORDS

(Accepted by the Federation Sportive Feminine International, October, 1930)

EVENT	RECORD	HOLDER AND NATION	WHERE MADE	YEAR
50 mtrs. run	.6 2-5s	Miss Mejzlikova II, Czechoslovakia	Paris	1922
		Miss Mejzlikova II, Czechoslovakia	Paris	1922
60 mtrs. run	7 3-5s	Miss Radideau, France	Stockholm	1926
		Miss Walasiewicz, Poland	Huta	1929
		Miss Mejzlikova II, Czechoslovakia	Paris	1922
80 mtrs. run	10s	Miss Radideau, France	Prague	1926
		Miss Gagneux, France	Paris	1929
100 mtrs. run	12s	Miss Cook, Canada	Halifax	1928
		Miss Schuurman, Holland	Amsterdam	1930
200 mtrs. run	24.7s	Kinuye Hitomi, Japan	Miyoshino	1929
800 mtrs. run	2m. 16 4-5s	Mrs. Lina Radke, Germany	Amsterdam	1928
1000 mtrs. run	3m. 8 1-5s	Miss Trickey, Great Britain	London	1924
80 mtrs. hurdles (8h)	12 1-5s	Miss Sychrova, Czechoslovakia	Prague	1928
		Miss Clark, South Africa	Durban	1930
300 mtrs. relay	38 4-5s	National Team, France	Prague	1926
	38 1-5s	Linnets Club, France	Paris	1929
400 mtrs. relay (4x100)	48 2-5s	National Team, Canada	Amsterdam	1928
	48.8s	Munich Club 1860, Germany	Nuremburg	1930
800 mtrs. relay (4x200)	1m. 47 3-5s	National Team, France	Paris	1929
		Linnets Club, France	Paris	1929
2400 mtrs. relay (3x800)	7m. 50s	Potsdamer Club Spf., Germany	Potsdam	1930
Running high jump	5 2656 ft. (1.605m)	Miss Gisolf, Holland	Maastricht	1929
Standing high jump	3.8057 ft. (1.16m)	Miss Dupuis, France	Paris	1925
Running broad jump	19.6191 ft. (5.98m)	Kinuye Hitomi, Japan	Osaka	1928
Standing broad jump	8 4316 ft. (2.57m)	Miss Holliday, Great Britain	London	1927
Shot put { best hand	42.1582 ft. (12 85m)	G Haublein, Germany	Frankfort	1929
{ two hands	70.4387 ft. (21 47m)	Miss Jungkunz, Germany	Ulm	1929
Discus { best hand	129 9852 ft. (39 62m)	Halinaa Konopacka, Poland	Amsterdam	1928
{ two hands	218.1139 ft. (66.485m)	Halinaa Konopacka, Poland	Warsaw	1928
Javelin { best hand	132.1178 ft. (40.27m)	E. Braumuller, Germany	Berlin	1930
{ two hands	187.1696 ft (57.05m)	Miss Haux, Germany	Ulm	1929
Tricathlon { 100 mtrs.	1.45s.			
217 pts. { High jump	4.7571 ft. (1.45m)	Kinuye Hitomi, Japan	Miyoshino	1929
{ Javelin	108 6929 ft. (33.13m)			

Bibliography

Aristophanes, translated by Benjamin Bickley Rogers. London, 1924.

Aristotle, Politics, translated by Benjamin Jowett. Oxford, 1908.

Arrianus, Flavius, translated by Edward James Chinnock. London, 1893.

Athenaeus, The Deipnosophists, translation by Charles Burton Gulick (Loeb ed.). New York, 1930.

Bury, J. B., History of Greece. London, 1924.

Cook, T. A., International Sport. London, 1908.

Coriolani, Christophori, de arte Gymnastica. Amsterdam, 1672. (Latin Text).

Duruy, Victor, History of Greece. London, 1892.

Gardiner, E. Norman, Greek Athletic Sports and Festivals. London, 1910.

Herodotus, translation by A. D. Godley (Loeb ed.). New York, 1924.

Herodotus, translation by George Rawlinson. London, 1875.

Hutton, Edward, A Glimpse of Greece. New York, 1928.

Hyde, Walter Woodburn, Olympic Victor Monuments and Greek Athletic Art. Washington, 1921.

King, Marian, The Story of Athletics. New York, 1931.

Lucian, Anacharsis, translation by A. M. Harmon (Loeb ed.). New York, 1925.

Mills, Dorothy, The Book of the Ancient Greeks. New York, 1925.

Pausanias, Description of Greece, translation by W. H. S. Jores and H. A. Ormerod (Loeb ed.). New York, 1926.

Philostratus. (Loeb edition). London, 1922.

Plato, Dialogues, translated by Benjamin Jowett. London, 1924.

Plutarch, Lives, translation by Bernadotte Perrin. (Loeb ed.). New York, 1914.

Reports of the American Olympic Committee for 1920, 1924 and 1928.

Robinson, James Harvey, The Mind in the Making. New York, 1921.

Sandys, Sir John, Pindar. London, 1924.

Smith, William, Dictionary of Greek and Roman Geography. London, 1857.

Socrates, Memorabilia, translated by E. C. Marchant. London, 1923.

Statius, Publius Papinius, translation by J. H. Mozley. (Loeb edition). London, 1928.

Thucydides, Translation by C. F. Smith (Loeb ed.). New York, 1921.

Webster, F. A. M., The Evolution of the Olympic Games. London, 1914.

Wells, H. G., The Outline of History. New York, 1922.

West, Gilbert, Dissertation on the Olympic Games (in his Pindar). London, 1749.

Xenophon, Hellenica and Anabasis. (Loeb edition). London, 1922.

Zervos, Skevos, Rhodes. Paris, 1920.

INDEX

Printed in the United States
122079LV00003B/15/A